path to purpose

A STUDY ON THE BOOK OF ECCLESIASTES

This study belongs to:

_____

_____

ALEXA HESS

Path to Purpose: A Study on the Book of Ecclesiastes
Copyright © 2023 by The Daily Grace Co.
Hanover, Maryland. All rights reserved.

Unless otherwise noted, all Scripture quotations are taken from the Christian Standard Bible®, Copyright © 2020 by Holman Bible Publishers. Used by permission. Christian Standard Bible® and CSB® are federally registered trademarks of Holman Bible Publishers.

The Daily Grace Co. exists to equip disciples to know and love God and His Word by creating beautiful, theologically rich, and accessible resources so that God may be glorified and the gospel made known.

Designed in the United States of America and printed in China.

Unlock Your Digital Study

*Did you know you can access your new study right from your phone?
Follow these simple steps, and you will be on your way to diving deeper into God's Word.*

Download The Daily Grace Co. App
AVAILABLE FOR FREE IN THE APP STORE AND GOOGLE PLAY.

Search for Your New Study
LOCATE YOUR STUDY IN THE DAILY GRACE CO. APP

- Select the "Studies" tab found at the bottom of the home page in the app.
- Select the pink "+" button to bring up all available studies.
- Click on your new study.

Apply Your Access Code
EMAILED TO YOU AFTER PURCHASE

- Copy the access code from your email, and enter it into the "Unlock Study with Access Code" box found on our app.
- You are all set! Now that you have downloaded the app, found your study, and applied your access code, you can begin your study virtually!
- If you did not receive an email with an access code after the purchase of your new study, check your spam folder. If you still cannot find your access code, contact our Customer Delight team at info@thedailygraceco.com.

OTHER APP FEATURES

VIDEOS COMMUNITY BIBLE BLOG PODCAST AND MORE!

Study Suggestions

We believe that the Bible is true, trustworthy, and timeless and that it is vitally important for all believers. These study suggestions are intended to help you more effectively study Scripture as you seek to know and love God through His Word.

SUGGESTED STUDY TOOLS

- ☐ Bible

- ☐ Double-spaced, printed copy of the Scripture passages that this study covers (You can use a website like www.biblegateway.com to copy the text of a passage and print out a double-spaced copy to be able to mark on easily.)

- ☐ Journal to write notes or prayers

- ☐ Six pens, colored pencils, or highlighters

- ☐ Dictionary to look up unfamiliar words

HOW TO USE THIS STUDY

Pray

Begin your study time in prayer. Ask God to reveal Himself to you, help you understand what you are reading, and transform you with His Word (Psalm 119:18).

Read Scripture

Before you read what is written in each day of the study itself, read the assigned passages of Scripture for that day. Use your double-spaced copy to circle, underline, highlight, draw arrows, and mark in any way you would like to help you dig deeper as you work through a passage.

Read Study Content

Read the daily written content provided for the current study day.

Respond

Answer the questions that appear at the end of each study day.

How to Study the Bible

The inductive method provides tools for deeper and more intentional Bible study.
To study the Bible inductively, work through the steps below after
reading background information on the book.

Observation & Comprehension
KEY QUESTION: WHAT DOES THE TEXT SAY?

After reading the daily Scripture in its entirety at least once, begin working with smaller portions of the Scripture. Read a passage of Scripture repetitively, and then mark the following items in the text:

- Key or repeated words and ideas
- Key themes
- Transition words (e.g., therefore, but, because, if/then, likewise, etc.)
- Lists
- Comparisons and contrasts
- Commands
- Unfamiliar words (look these up in a dictionary)
- Questions you have about the text

Interpretation
KEY QUESTION: WHAT DOES THE TEXT MEAN?

Once you have annotated the text, work through the following steps to help you interpret its meaning:

- Read the passage in other versions for a better understanding of the text.
- Read cross-references to help interpret Scripture with Scripture.
- Paraphrase or summarize the passage to check for understanding.
- Identify how the text reflects the metanarrative of Scripture, which is the story of creation, fall, redemption, and restoration.
- Read trustworthy commentaries if you need further insight into the meaning of the passage.

Application
KEY QUESTION: HOW SHOULD THE TRUTH OF THIS PASSAGE CHANGE ME?

Bible study is not merely an intellectual pursuit. The truths about God, ourselves, and the gospel that we discover in Scripture should produce transformation in our hearts and lives. Answer the following questions and prompts as you consider what you have learned in your study:

- What attributes of God's character are revealed in the passage?
- Consider places where the text directly states the character of God, as well as how His character is revealed through His words and actions.
- What do I learn about myself in light of who God is?
- Consider how you fall short of God's character, how the text reveals your sin nature, and what it says about your new identity in Christ.
- How should this truth change me?
- A passage of Scripture may contain direct commands telling us what to do or warnings about sins to avoid in order to help us grow in holiness. Other times, our application flows out of seeing ourselves in light of God's character. As we pray and reflect on how God is calling us to change in light of His Word, we should be asking questions like, "How should I pray for God to change my heart?" and "What practical steps can I take toward cultivating habits of holiness?"

The Attributes of God

Eternal
God has no beginning and no end. He always was, always is, and always will be.
HAB. 1:12 / REV. 1:8 / IS. 41:4

Faithful
God is incapable of anything but fidelity. He is loyally devoted to His plan and purpose.
2 TIM. 2:13 / DEUT. 7:9 / HEB. 10:23

Good
God is pure; there is no defilement in Him. He is unable to sin, and all He does is good.
GEN. 1:31 / PS. 34:8 / PS. 107:1

Gracious
God is kind, giving us gifts and benefits we do not deserve.
**2 KINGS 13:23 / PS. 145:8
IS. 30:18**

Holy
God is undefiled and unable to be in the presence of defilement. He is sacred and set-apart.
REV. 4:8 / LEV. 19:2 / HAB. 1:13

Incomprehensible and Transcendent
God is high above and beyond human understanding. He is unable to be fully known.
**PS. 145:3 / IS. 55:8-9
ROM. 11:33-36**

Immutable
God does not change. He is the same yesterday, today, and tomorrow.
**1 SAM. 15:29 / ROM. 11:29
JAMES 1:17**

Infinite
God is limitless. He exhibits all of His attributes perfectly and boundlessly.
**ROM. 11:33-36 / IS. 40:28
PS. 147:5**

Jealous
God is desirous of receiving the praise and affection He rightly deserves.
**EX. 20:5 / DEUT. 4:23-24
JOSH. 24:19**

Just
God governs in perfect justice. He acts in accordance with justice. In Him, there is no wrongdoing or dishonesty.
IS. 61:8 / DEUT. 32:4 / PS. 146:7-9

Loving
God is eternally, enduringly, steadfastly loving and affectionate. He does not forsake or betray His covenant love.
JN. 3:16 / EPH. 2:4-5 / 1 JN. 4:16

Merciful
God is compassionate, withholding from us the wrath that we deserve.
**TITUS 3:5 / PS. 25:10
LAM. 3:22-23**

Omnipotent
God is all-powerful; His strength is unlimited.
MAT. 19:26 / JOB 42:1-2
JER. 32:27

Omnipresent
God is everywhere; His presence is near and permeating.
PROV. 15:3 / PS. 139:7-10
JER. 23:23-24

Omniscient
God is all-knowing; there is nothing unknown to Him.
PS. 147:4 / I JN. 3:20
HEB. 4:13

Patient
God is long-suffering and enduring. He gives ample opportunity for people to turn toward Him.
ROM. 2:4 / 2 PET. 3:9 / PS. 86:15

Self-Existent
God was not created but exists by His power alone.
PS. 90:1-2 / JN. 1:4 / JN. 5:26

Self-Sufficient
God has no needs and depends on nothing, but everything depends on God.
IS. 40:28-31 / ACTS 17:24-25
PHIL. 4:19

Sovereign
God governs over all things; He is in complete control.
COL. 1:17 / PS. 24:1-2
1 CHRON. 29:11-12

Truthful
God is our measurement of what is fact. By Him we are able to discern true and false.
JN. 3:33 / ROM. 1:25 / JN. 14:6

Wise
God is infinitely knowledgeable and is judicious with His knowledge.
IS. 46:9-10 / IS. 55:9 / PROV. 3:19

Wrathful
God stands in opposition to all that is evil. He enacts judgment according to His holiness, righteousness, and justice.
PS. 69:24 / JN. 3:36 / ROM. 1:18

Timeline of Scripture

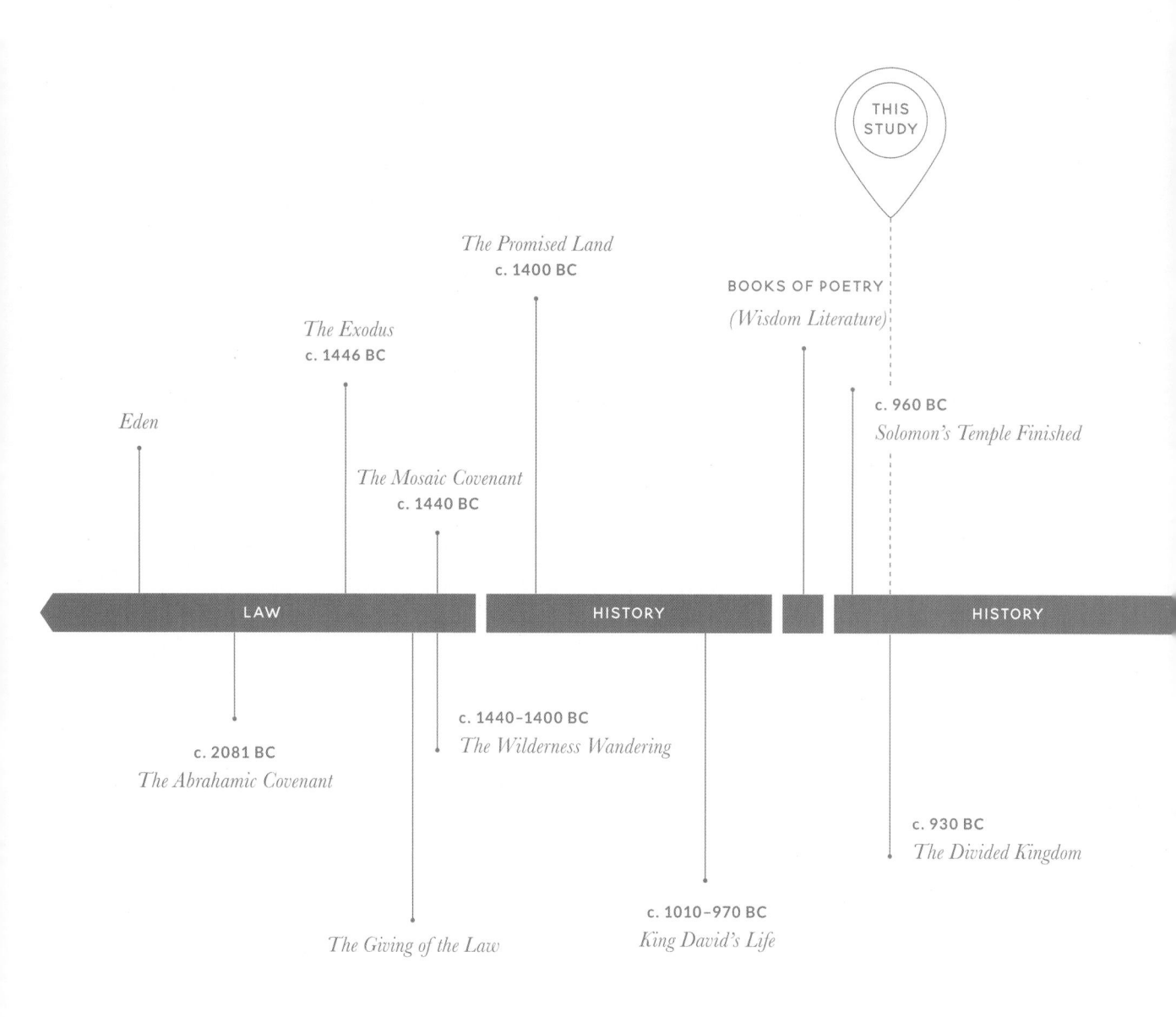

THIS STUDY

Eden

c. 2081 BC
The Abrahamic Covenant

The Exodus
c. 1446 BC

The Giving of the Law

The Mosaic Covenant
c. 1440 BC

The Promised Land
c. 1400 BC

c. 1440–1400 BC
The Wilderness Wandering

c. 1010–970 BC
King David's Life

BOOKS OF POETRY
(Wisdom Literature)

c. 960 BC
Solomon's Temple Finished

c. 930 BC
The Divided Kingdom

LAW | HISTORY | HISTORY

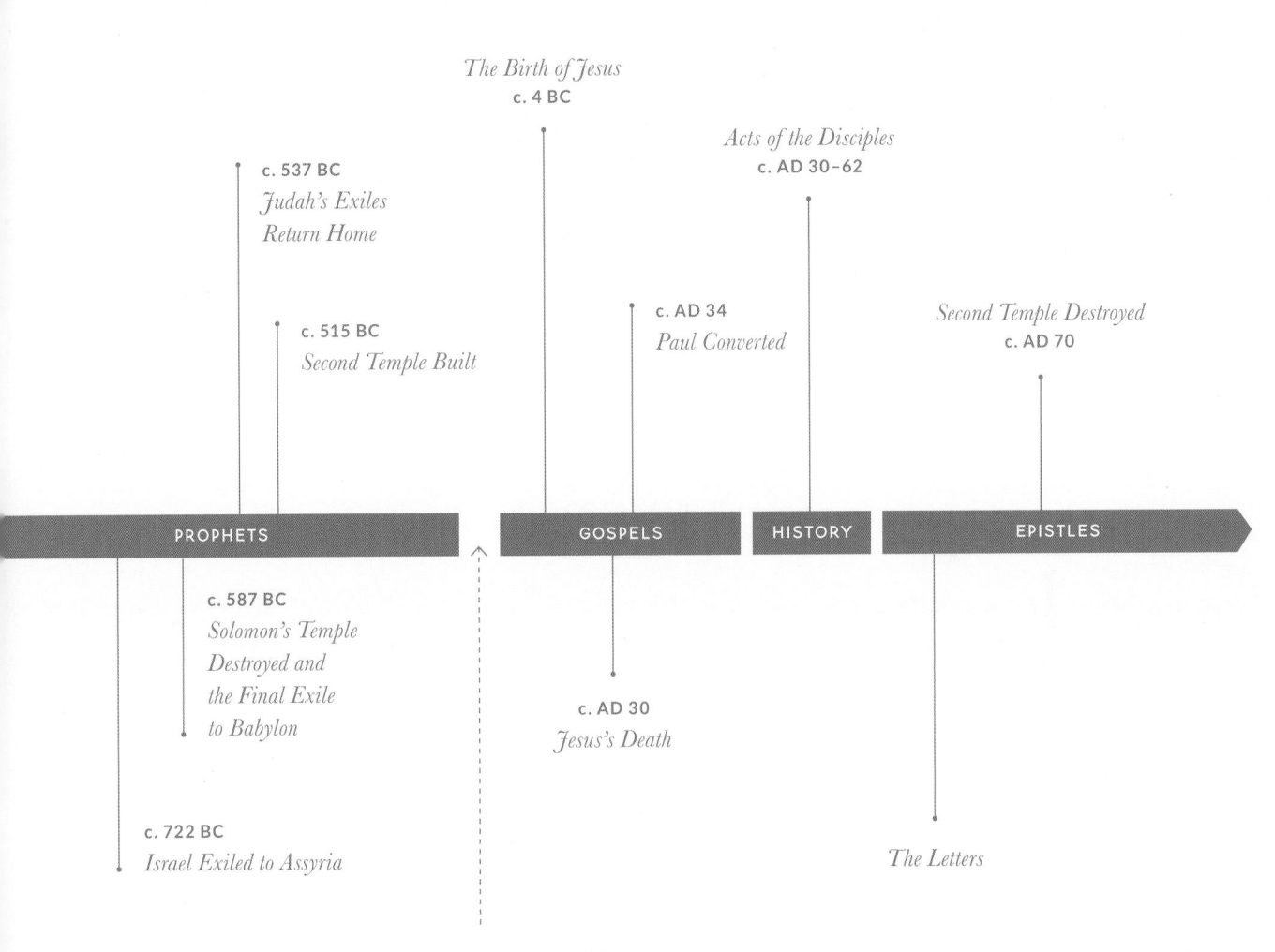

The Birth of Jesus
c. 4 BC

Acts of the Disciples
c. AD 30–62

c. 537 BC
*Judah's Exiles
Return Home*

Second Temple Destroyed
c. AD 70

c. 515 BC
Second Temple Built

c. AD 34
Paul Converted

| PROPHETS | GOSPELS | HISTORY | EPISTLES |

c. 587 BC
*Solomon's Temple
Destroyed and
the Final Exile
to Babylon*

c. AD 30
Jesus's Death

The Letters

c. 722 BC
Israel Exiled to Assyria

The Intertestamental Period

TIMELINE OF SCRIPTURE • 11

Metanarrative of Scripture

Creation

In the beginning, God created the universe. He made the world and everything in it. He created humans in His own image to be His representatives on the earth.

Fall

The first humans, Adam and Eve, disobeyed God by eating from the fruit of the Tree of Knowledge of Good and Evil. Their disobedience impacted the whole world. The punishment for sin is death, and because of Adam's original sin, all humans are sinful and condemned to death.

Redemption

God sent His Son to become a human and redeem His people. Jesus Christ lived a sinless life but died on the cross to pay the penalty for sin. He resurrected from the dead and ascended into heaven. All who put their faith in Jesus are saved from death and freely receive the gift of eternal life.

Restoration

One day, Jesus Christ will return again and restore all that sin destroyed. He will usher in a new heaven and new earth where all who trust in Him will live eternally with glorified bodies in the presence of God.

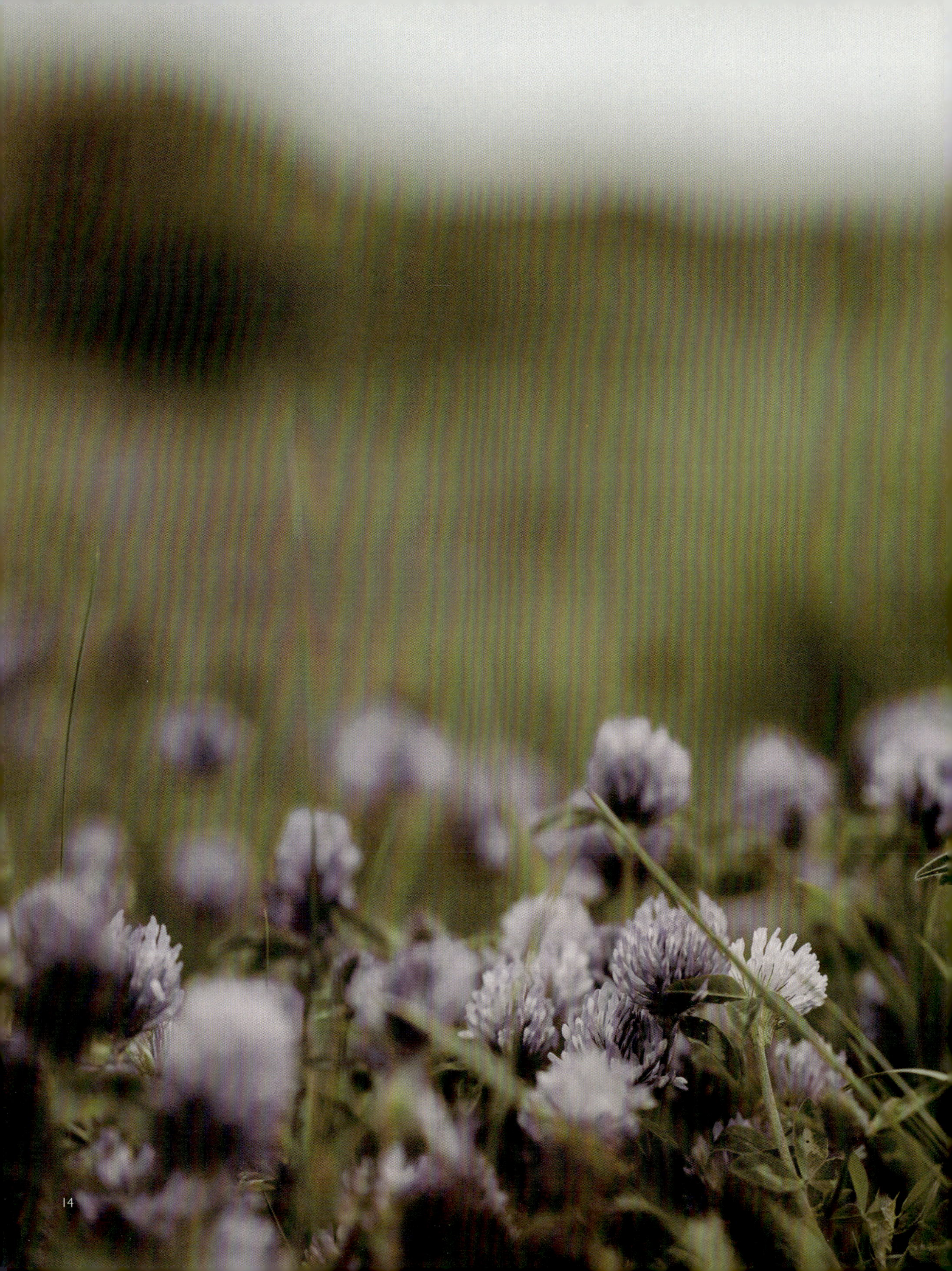

In This Study

Intro

3	Unlock Your Digital Study
4	Study Suggestions
6	How to Study the Bible
8	The Attributes of God
10	Timeline of Scripture
12	Metanarrative of Scripture

Week One

16	Day One
48	Scripture Memory
50	Week One Reflection

Week Two

52	Day One
82	Scripture Memory
84	Week Two Reflection

Week Three

86	Day One
116	Scripture Memory
118	Week Three Reflection

Extras

22	How to Read and Interpret Wisdom Literature
120	Solomon as a Type of Christ
124	What is the Gospel?

Without Jesus, there is no hope for this world or meaning in this life, which is what Ecclesiastes shows us.

week one day one

A Frustrating Quest

READ ECCLESIASTES 1–12

A man sets out on a journey. He does not have all the details of this trip planned, but he does know what he is looking for—happiness and satisfaction. First, he tries a road marked "wisdom and knowledge," and while he experiences some delight along the way, eventually, the road leads to a dead end. He turns around and tries another path called "riches and glory," but this path ends the same as the first. Frustrated, he tries a path called "the fruits of labor," but sadly, this path leads to a dead end as well.

We are no different from the man in this situation. Each of us sets out on a journey of discovery, a journey to find answers and experience the destination our hearts desire. But without our compass, we reach a dead end each time. The book of Ecclesiastes describes this journey that each of us takes. It reveals the insights of someone who sought to discover the meaning of life and what makes life worth living. Ecclesiastes describes this man's frustrations with each pursuit that results in a dead end. Who is this man?

This man is traditionally believed to be Solomon. The book of Ecclesiastes opens with "the words of the Teacher, son of David, king in Jerusalem" (Ecclesiastes 1:1). The name given, "the Teacher,"

Reading Ecclesiastes focuses our eyes on our need for Christ.

is where the title "Ecclesiastes" comes from. The Hebrew word for Ecclesiastes is the word *Qōhelet*, which translates as "preacher" or "teacher." The word *Qōhelet* describes someone who addresses an assembly. This title, as well as the title of "son of David, king in Jerusalem," strongly points to Solomon, who was David's son and became king over Israel. However, most scholars agree that the words of Ecclesiastes are likely from an editor who presents the teachings of Solomon. This editor probably took the lessons of Solomon's life and wrote them, intending to teach readers the wisdom gleaned from Solomon's experiences.

The purpose of imparting wisdom and knowledge causes Ecclesiastes to fall into the genre of wisdom literature. Scholars have disagreed over the years about how to interpret the wisdom of Ecclesiastes. Some believe the main takeaway is a pessimistic view of life, whereas others believe it provides an optimistic view. Some assume Solomon is a skeptic who takes an irreligious point of view, while others assume that Solomon is a believer who teaches about faithfulness to God. But as the years have passed, scholars tend to agree that Ecclesiastes is an apologetic essay, meaning that it is a defense for faith in God.

The author accomplishes this purpose by describing Solomon's thoughts, feelings, and experiences that reveal life's grimness without a relationship with God. The negativity, positivity, skepticism, and faith in the book of Ecclesiastes portray an accurate picture of humanity's quest for truth and meaning. Like Solomon, we too struggle to understand how this world works and the purpose of our existence. We wrestle with questions about God, suffering, injustice, and the future. Solomon tackles these struggles and questions in Ecclesiastes. Through it all, Solomon seeks to give readers a realistic perspective on the brokenness of this world and how one can still live with hope and joy in a dark and fleeting world.

While reading Ecclesiastes, it is important to keep in mind where Solomon was in redemptive history. During his life and reign as king, Israel was in a covenantal relationship with God. Israel was experiencing the fulfillment of God's promise to bring them to the Promised Land and grow them into a thriving nation. God had also promised a deliverer who would crush the enemy (Genesis 3:15), and God expanded on this promise through the covenant He made with Solomon's father, David. God promised that from David's line would come a king who would deliver His people and rule over an eternal kingdom. The people of Israel, Solomon included, hoped for this coming Messiah. Many years later, this coming Messiah would be revealed as Jesus, but for now, the nation of Israel waited for God's promise to be fulfilled.

Because Solomon lived before Jesus came, Solomon did not know the whole picture of God's redemptive plan. We should remember this reality as we read verses in which Solomon wrestles with questions about the meaning of life and what lies beyond death. At times, we may be frustrated that Solomon does not seem to always give us answers to his questions. However, the open-ended nature of some of Solomon's questions reveals the need for Jesus and an eternal perspective. Without Jesus, there is no hope for this world or meaning in this life, which is what Ecclesiastes shows us.

Ecclesiastes points us to our need for Jesus by describing different aspects of this world that appear futile or meaningless. These areas include work, riches, and possessions. Solomon also speaks about the themes of injustice, wickedness, and death to teach about the brokenness of our world. In reading Ecclesiastes, we may find ourselves feeling downcast and disheartened, but these feelings are necessary in that it is good for us to realize how the world is broken and how the pursuits we often chase will not save or satisfy us. When all else is taken away, we can see our need for God more clearly.

Therefore, the journey Solomon makes in Ecclesiastes acts as a warning to readers. The dead ends Solomon finds in his pursuit of happiness and satisfaction warn readers not to follow down the same paths. In the end, Solomon's experiences reveal that we need our compass, God, who gives us guidance to follow the path to life. Ultimately, the path to life is found in Jesus Christ. It is salvation through Jesus that secures us with eternal life and enables us to live the fullness of life in the present. Reading Ecclesiastes focuses our eyes on our need for Christ and teaches us how nothing else in this world can save or satisfy us but Jesus.

study questions

What key words or themes stood out to you while reading Ecclesiastes?

_____

_____

_____

_____

_____

_____

study questions

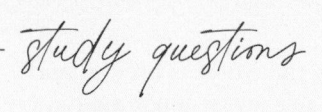

What feelings or emotions did you experience while reading Ecclesiastes?

Summarize the book of Ecclesiastes below.

Notes

extra

How to Read and Interpret Wisdom Literature

The Book of Ecclesiastes falls into the genre of wisdom literature. Wisdom literature provides principles on how to live wisely in the world. Wisdom literature typically involves poetry and proverbs. Poetry uses figurative language to communicate abstract truths. Proverbs are short statements that state a general truth or word of wisdom. It is important to remember that the poetry and proverbs found in wisdom literature should be interpreted figuratively rather than literally. Proverbs are not always universally applicable and should be seen as principles more than promises.

Unlike the wisdom literature of other texts, wisdom literature in the Bible is designed to teach readers how to obey God and walk in His ways. The poetry and proverbs in wisdom literature are meant to be more memorable than theologically accurate. Instead of teaching doctrine, wisdom literature typically emphasizes theological application in certain areas of life. At times, certain proverbs or sayings in wisdom literature may appear contradictory to one another or even other passages of Scripture. This is why it is important to interpret wisdom literature in light of the book as a whole, other wisdom literature in Scripture, and the entirety of the Bible.

Devices Used in Wisdom Literature

SYNONYMOUS PARALLELISM
By varying the language, the second part of a phrase repeats what has been expressed in the first part of a phrase

ANTITHETICAL PARALLELISM
The first part of a phrase contrasts with the second part of a phrase to communicate two different ideas

ALLEGORY
A story, poem, or picture that reveals a hidden moral or political meaning

PERSONIFICATION
Giving a non-human thing human characteristics

METAPHOR
Describing an object in a way that is not literally true in order to make a comparison

SYNECDOCHE
A part is made to represent the whole

The seeming meaninglessness of life points us to the truth that only Jesus gives our lives true meaning.

week one day two

Everything is Futile

READ ECCLESIASTES 1:1–11

Some movies open with a cheery mood—the sun shining bright, the birds chirping, and an upbeat song playing in the background. Ecclesiastes does not begin this way. Instead of a joyful opening, Solomon opens with these jarring words: "Absolute futility. Everything is futile" (Ecclesiastes 1:2). These opening words may tempt us to close the book and pick up something more encouraging. But this phrase from Solomon is an important message to grasp before the book continues. Everything in this world is futile, which points us to the truth that there is something more to this life than what the world can bring us.

The English word "futile" means something that is "pointless or meaningless." However, the word "futile" in Hebrew is *hebel*, which means "vapor" or "breath." Solomon likely uses this word to teach from the very beginning how the things of this world are like vapor. You can see a vapor of smoke or one's breath in the chilly air, but you cannot grasp the air. In comparison, the things of this world seem tangible, but when you try to grasp them, you will find that you cannot hold onto them. From the start, Solomon reveals the empty pursuit of worldly loves. Everything we seek to acquire in this life—beauty, fame, fortune—will fail us and fade away.

There is more to this life, for true and lasting life is found in Jesus Christ.

Solomon continues by briefly presenting one of the major themes of Ecclesiastes in verse 3 — the futility of labor. He asks the question, "What does a person gain for all his efforts that he labors at under the sun?" At first glance, we may find Solomon's question strange. Our labor does produce something, whether it be money in the bank account or a product we have made. Yet Solomon seems to say we do not gain or profit from our labor. Why?

The phrase "under the sun" sheds some light on an answer. The phrase "under the sun" is a phrase Solomon utilizes multiple times throughout Ecclesiastes. This phrase communicates an earthly perspective — that one is gathering such an opinion about the futility of labor by looking at what they observe in the world alone. Labor is, in fact, futile if there is nothing beyond this world. If this life is all there is, nothing we produce has any lasting value or impact.

To further communicate this truth, Solomon describes nature's rhythms in verses 4–7. He explains how generations are born and eventually die, but the earth remains. He describes the sun as a hurried runner who works hard to rise and circle around, but eventually, it returns to where it began. The wind also seems like it does much as it gusts all around the earth, but it also returns to its designed cycle. The streams that flow into the sea may seem like their waters contribute much, but even with the stream's flow, the sea is never full.

Solomon continues to describe the futility of this world in verse 8 by saying how our words, eyes, and ears are never satisfied. In verses 9–10, Solomon reveals how there is nothing new under the sun. There is not anything we can point to and say that it is new. Every new advancement or product contains some element that has always existed. What we consider new falls into the cycle of futility, for even what is new eventually fades and is replaced by something else. Lastly, Solomon says in verse 11 that there is no remembrance of one's life. Even those who have been remembered for something they have done in the past will soon fade from memory.

Solomon's words in this passage reveal the reality of our lives. We, too, are caught in a seemingly endless rhythm. We only need to look at our daily lives to see how this is true. We all get up and have a morning ritual that involves brushing our teeth or drinking coffee. Then we set off to do what the day requires as we go to work, take the kids to school, or begin to clean our home. Eventually, time goes on, and we finish our day. Climbing back into bed, we will rise tomorrow to repeat the same rhythm. Even if we feel like we have achieved something in this routine, life always seems to reset itself. We finish our work one day but have to start more work the next. The pile of laundry has been washed, dried, and put away, but soon the basket will fill again. The refrigerator may be stocked for now, but soon the food will dwindle, and another grocery run will ensue.

Realizing life's seemingly mundane and meaningless nature may prompt us to throw up our hands in frustration. "What is the point?" we might ask. But this is the question Solomon has asked himself before and what he wants his readers to ask as well. While others may choose to ignore the reality of this life, coming to terms with this reality sets us on the right path of discovery. The seeming meaninglessness of life points us to the truth that only Jesus gives our lives true meaning. The desire for there to be something more to this life is fulfilled in Christ alone.

As humans, we were created to fulfill one purpose: to love and worship God. Sin causes this purpose to be disrupted and diluted. But through the grace and forgiveness of Jesus, our eyes are opened back to our true purpose. Because of Jesus, we can participate in the cycles of this life with joy rather than despair. We can complete the seemingly mundane with delight, knowing that the work of our hands gives God glory. We can look ahead with hope because of our future of eternity with Christ. There is more to this life, for true and lasting life is found in Jesus Christ.

study questions

What are some things of this world (beauty, fortune, fame, etc.) that you tend to pursue?

_____

_____

_____

_____

_____

_____

study questions

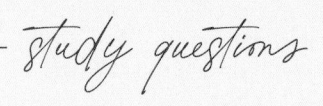

Why is it important to realize that the things of this world are like vapor? How can this truth impact your day-to-day life?

_____
_____
_____
_____
_____
_____
_____
_____
_____

How can dissatisfaction point you to Jesus and your purpose in Him?

_____
_____
_____
_____
_____
_____
_____
_____
_____
_____
_____

Notes

It is only through a relationship with God, given to us through Jesus, that we find true life and purpose.

week one day three

Pursuits of the Wind

READ ECCLESIASTES 1:12–2:26

Solomon has revealed to us the futility of life according to his observations from nature, and now he reveals the futility of life through his experiences. In this passage, Solomon takes us down four paths he followed on his quest for meaning: wisdom, pleasure, possessions, and labor. As we journey down these paths with Solomon, we continue to see how the pursuits of this world do not give us answers to our hearts' questions and longings. Instead, they only leave us searching.

Solomon starts by reiterating his title of king over Israel. His quest is presented here clearly as he describes his desire to make sense of the world during his reign. Solomon describes how God has given mankind this quest for meaning to keep them occupied. On the surface, these words seem to present God as a cruel jokester who desires to confuse His creation. However, we must remember that Solomon presents his findings through the lens of a worldly perspective. Soon, he will give us a theological perspective, but for now, he reveals to us how examining life under the sun alone is a frustrating and restless quest.

Solomon explains this further as he describes his path of wisdom. If you have read other wisdom literature in the Bible, such as the book of Proverbs, you

> It is the life of faith given to us through Christ that brings us true satisfaction.

would likely expect the teachings about wisdom in Ecclesiastes to be positive. However, Solomon seems to negatively view wisdom in this passage. Nevertheless, Solomon sees value in wisdom enough to continue to apply it throughout his quest. As he goes on to discuss the path of pleasure in Ecclesiastes 2:3, he includes how his mind still guides him with wisdom. This verse reveals how Solomon still employs an element of caution and consideration as he explores pleasures that are unwise. Yet even though Solomon allows himself to experience what is good and pleasurable to man, this pursuit is revealed to be futile once again. Solomon shows how the pleasures of life do not solve the problems of life when he says, "it is madness," and asks, "what does this accomplish?" (Ecclesiastes 2:2).

Solomon goes on in Ecclesiastes 2:4–11 to teach about the futility of possessions. On the path of possessions, Solomon acquires houses and vineyards, servants, livestock, silver and gold, singers, and concubines. These achievements cause him to become great and more successful than the kings who reigned before him. Although Solomon does not deny himself anything his eyes desire, he still finds himself dissatisfied. Just like the previous paths, the path of possessions is futile.

The failure of these pursuits causes Solomon to turn back to wisdom. In his decision to indulge in madness and folly, or sinful and unwise choices, he realizes the advantage of wisdom. In Ecclesiastes 2:13, Solomon describes this advantage as light over darkness. He includes a proverb in Ecclesiastes 2:14 that teaches how a wise person can see clearly, but a fool is blind. In the Bible's wisdom literature, the fool represents someone who does not follow God, and the wise person represents someone who does follow God. Even though Solomon sees the benefit of wisdom, he is bothered by the fate of the fool and the wise because both will experience death. This reality causes Solomon to hate life, for, on the surface, it appears as if there is no earthly benefit for the wise if they too face the same fate as the fool.

Solomon goes on to explain his hatred of work in Ecclesiastes 2:18–23. He describes his frustration that when one dies, their work is handed down to those who come after them. Even if one works hard in their life, there is no promise that those who pick up their work after them will do so with wisdom. Similar to his words from the previous passage, Solomon says that a laborer does not truly gain from his efforts. Though he works tirelessly, there is no rest for him.

Yet hope bursts forth in Ecclesiastes 2:24. Solomon says that one can view their work and the pleasures of life, such as eating and drinking, as a gift from God. If this life is all there is, our work and even simple joys are meaningless. But because everything is a gift from God, we can delight in these things. Yet Solomon also reminds us that we should not delight in God's gifts as our ultimate joy. He asks in Ecclesiastes 2:25 who can enjoy life apart from God. His words here teach us how true life is found in God alone. It is only through a relationship with Him that we are given the ability to see this world through the lens of the gospel and enjoy the gifts God has given us.

This relationship with God is only available through Jesus Christ. When we repent and trust in Jesus, we are forgiven of our sins and given a relationship with God. The gifts of wisdom, knowledge, and joy that Solomon lists in Ecclesiastes 2:26 are granted to those saved by Christ's grace. It is only through a relationship with God, given to us through Jesus, that we find true life and purpose.

Today's passage teaches us how worldly pursuits leave us empty-handed, but pursuing the Lord amounts to great gain. Solomon will teach further about a life of faith, but for now, his words reveal the futility of life apart from God. This passage leaves us with a choice to make. Will we live a life of worldly pursuits that only perpetuate our dissatisfaction? Or will we turn to Jesus and embrace the life that is found in Him? Worldly wisdom, empty pleasures, possessions, and labor cannot and will not satisfy us. It is the life of faith given to us through Christ that brings us true satisfaction.

study questions

How do you see the world chase after worldly wisdom, pleasures, possessions, and labor as a source of meaning and satisfaction? How can you keep yourself from chasing the same pursuits?

_____
_____
_____
_____
_____
_____
_____

study questions

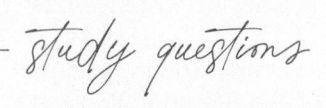

Read Psalm 104. According to this psalm, what should our response be to the gifts that God has given us?

_____
_____
_____
_____
_____
_____
_____
_____
_____

What does it say about God's character that He gives us good gifts and life through Christ?

_____
_____
_____
_____
_____
_____
_____
_____
_____
_____
_____
_____
_____

Notes

We can rejoice and enjoy this life as we trust in the God who holds our lives in His hands.

week one day four

A Time for Everything

READ ECCLESIASTES 3:1–15

Our years are marked by seasons. Chilly winter, sweet spring, sunny summer, crisp fall. These seasons have a regular rhythm over which we have no control, coming and going according to God's perfect timing. This idea of rhythm and time is what Solomon explores in this passage. As Solomon examines the mystery of time and the regular rhythms of life, he teaches us important insight to help us trust in the sovereignty of God.

Solomon opens this passage by describing how there is an appointed time for everything in this world. The verses that follow make up a chiasm, a poetic structure used in many passages of the Bible. In chiastic poetry, ideas are presented and then repeated in reverse. Some scholars believe this poem specifically makes contrasts between what is desirable and what is undesirable. For example, in verse 2, birth is typically desirable, whereas death is typically undesirable. The second line in the verse repeats this pattern. Planting is desirable because it yields a harvest, but a time to uproot can be undesirable because it likely means the plant is dead. Verses 3–8 continue to follow this chiastic pattern, contrasting what is perhaps desirable with what is perhaps undesirable.

> May we place our lives in the hands of our God, whose timing is always perfect.

We do not know for sure if the intent of this poem was to describe what is desirable versus undesirable. We do know that Solomon is using these examples to teach how certain events and activities seem to occur at certain times. As we look at the list of different activities, we can see how these examples come to play in our own lives. There are moments when we laugh and moments when we cry. There are times when we purchase items and times when we get rid of items. There are times when we rejoice over life and times when we mourn over death. While humans have some control over the events of seasons, there are some seasons in which we cannot control what occurs. But even though we cannot control the activities and events in certain seasons, we can control how we respond.

Solomon goes on in verse 11 to say how God has made everything appropriate, or beautiful, in its time. This verse describes how there is a creative order to God's design. God is the One who providentially controls all of creation and appoints events and seasons according to His sovereignty. Solomon explains how God has put eternity in man's heart, which means He has given man the ability to desire something eternal. Yet this ability is limited. Humans are limited in their understanding when it comes to the sovereign work of God.

This longing to understand what is beyond what we can see and discern gives all of us a sense of restlessness. We can feel the limits of our understanding and become frustrated that we cannot fully grasp God's plan and how He works. This can either cause us to turn away from God in bitterness or turn toward Him in trust. Limitations are a gift from God because God uses our limitations to draw us to Himself. Our limits point us to our need for God, who has no limits. When we come to terms with the fact that we cannot fully understand how this world works and what the future holds, we are able to surrender our control to God. We might not know all things, but God does, so we can trust Him.

In verses 12–13, Solomon again discusses his previous statements from chapter 2 about the pleasures of life that God has given mankind. This time, however, Solomon speaks of them in relation to the sovereignty of God. We can rejoice and enjoy this life as we trust in the God who holds our lives in His hands. Solomon also teaches in verse 14 how the sovereign works of God are meant to cause humans to be in awe of Him. When we look at the mysterious and marvelous way God works, we are led to worship Him.

The mystery of time and the regular rhythms of life should lead us to trust God. While God has given humanity the ability to make decisions, we do not have ultimate control over our lives. It can be hard to acknowledge and surrender this lack of control over fear of how the circumstances of our lives will unfold. We might not know the whole story of our lives—but God does. In the moments we struggle to trust God's plans, we must look to the story of the gospel.

From the very beginning, God put forth a plan to save humanity from their sin. God's people were given some details but not the entire picture of how this plan would unfold. Yet, in His faithfulness, God saw His plan to completion. Thousands of years later, God's redemptive plan was fulfilled in Christ. Paul, the author of the New Testament book of Galatians, explains this when he writes, "When the time came to completion, God sent His Son, born of a woman, born under the law, to redeem those under the law, so that we might receive adoption as sons" (Galatians 4:4–5). In His perfect timing, God sent Jesus, who lived a perfect life and died the death we all deserve for our sins. Jesus rose from the dead three days later, declaring victory over sin and death.

Because God accomplished His plan of redemption through Christ, we can trust that He will accomplish His plans for our lives. We might not know all the workings of our story, but we can trust the author who has written the pages. And for those of us in Christ, we know the end of the story. We know that one day Christ will return to make all things new. Until then, may we place our lives in the hands of our God, whose timing is always perfect.

study questions

How do you struggle with trusting God's timing?

_____
_____
_____
_____
_____
_____
_____

study questions

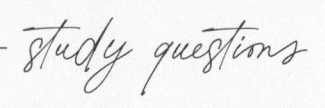

How do you view your limitations? How can your limits lead you to trust God?

How does the sovereignty of God impact our worship? Write out a prayer, praising God for who He is and how He works.

Notes

Solomon's perspective on death and injustice reveals that there is no hope without the gospel's message.

week one day five

God Will Judge

READ ECCLESIASTES 3:16–22

When we look at the world around us, we can become easily discouraged. There are people in poverty, children in the foster care system, corrupt leaders, and the list continues. The weightiness of injustice can cause us to ask, "When Lord? When will you make things right?" This question, as well as the reality of death, is what Solomon explores in today's passage. Solomon ended the previous passage by saying how God seeks justice for the persecuted. Death may be a reality, and injustice may be all around us, but we have a judge who imparts life and promises to set all things right.

Solomon opens this passage by observing injustice. He mourns over the fact that at the place of justice, the courts, there is injustice. Sadly, we can see how our current courts are no different. While some laws and regulations have contributed to the well-being of mankind, other regulations have not. There have been laws that allow murder, leaders who thrive on power, and people who are wrongly accused and imprisoned. It can break our hearts to look at a system that is supposed to execute justice and instead see injustice. Yet Solomon brings this hope to the reality of injustice—God has an appointed time for judgment. God is not ignorant to injustice, nor does He turn a blind eye. God sees

> The gospel gives us hope for the future, but the gospel also gives us hope for the present.

all injustice, and He has an appointed time when He will punish the wicked and right every wrong.

Solomon then examines the subject of death in verses 19–20. He reveals how both animals and mankind share the same fate—death. Because they both experience death, Solomon says people do not have any advantage over animals. All come from dust, and all will return to dust. This language of dust echoes the consequence God gave Adam and Eve when they sinned. God declared in Genesis 3:19, "For you are dust, and you will return to dust." The consequence of death is connected to sin. Sin deserves to be punished, and because all humanity sins, all humans deserve the punishment of death.

Solomon continues the subject of death by explaining how no one knows what lies beyond death. From Solomon's perspective, there is no certainty whether people or animals go upward to meet God or downward away from Him. Yet Solomon connects this limitation with the importance of enjoying the gifts of this current life. Even though no one can see what happens beyond death, the reality of death can cause one to take hold of the life they have in the present.

Solomon's perspective on death and injustice reveals that there is no hope without the gospel's message. Solomon's observations about injustice and death reflect his previous observations; that is, they are developed from what he examines with his eyes. With his limited perspective, Solomon claims that no one can observe the workings of this world and know for certain if there is hope for injustice or a life beyond death. The open-ended questions Solomon presents in this passage, as well as his limited perspective, reveal how we need the message of the gospel. The gospel answers our questions about suffering and what lies beyond death. Not only this, but the gospel also gives us solutions.

Though Adam and Eve brought death for all creation, God brought life through Christ. The work of Christ on the cross forgives the sin that condemns us and gives us eternal life with God. This gift of eternal life causes us to observe death with the right perspective. As believers, we know for certain that on the other side of death is eternal life with God in heaven. Our salvation through Christ also gives us security for God's future judgment. While both believers and unbelievers will stand before God in judgment, the grace of Christ declares believers innocent. However, those who do not believe in Jesus will be sentenced to eternal separation from God.

The gospel gives us hope for the future, but the gospel also gives us hope for the present. If this life were all there is, there would be no solution for suffering and injustice. But God's redemptive plan involves reversing the curse that sin created. When Christ returns and God's judgment is carried out, all wrongdoing will be made right.

All evil activity that is done under the sun will be punished, and God will transform the world back to a place of perfect righteousness.

As we continue to live in our broken world, we trust in our righteous Judge. We reflect our just God as we serve the poor, do what is right, and contribute to the flourishing of creation. And as we wait for the day when Christ will make all things new, we have the opportunity to answer the questions people have about injustice and death. In Christ, there is life, peace, and eternal hope.

> "When Christ returns and God's judgment is carried out, all wrongdoing will be made right."

study questions

How does the gospel bring peace to those who fear death?

_____
_____
_____
_____
_____
_____
_____

study questions

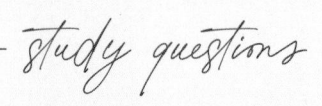

How does knowing God will make all things right give you comfort today?

_____
_____
_____
_____
_____
_____
_____
_____
_____
_____

In what ways can you act justly as a follower of Christ?

_____
_____
_____
_____
_____
_____
_____
_____
_____
_____
_____
_____

Notes

Scripture Memory

week one day six

There is nothing better for a person than to eat, drink, and enjoy his work. I have seen that even this is from God's hand, because who can eat and who can enjoy life apart from him?

ECCLESIASTES 2:24–25

Week One *Reflection*

Summarize the main points from this week's passages.

What did you observe from this week's text about God and His character?

What did these passages teach you about the condition of mankind and yourself?

READ ECCLESIASTES 1:1–3:22

How did these passages point to the gospel?

_____

_____

_____

_____

How should you respond to these passages?
What specific action steps can you take this week to apply them in your life?

_____

_____

_____

_____

Write a prayer in response to your study of God's Word. Adore God for who He is, confess sins He revealed in your own life, ask Him to empower you to walk in obedience, and pray for anyone who comes to mind as you study.

_____

_____

_____

_____

_____

It is the grace and forgiveness of Christ that brings healing to the broken places of this world.

week two day one

Four Problems and Pursuits of the Wind

READ ECCLESIASTES 4

Solomon has been taking us on a journey through the observations he has made during his life. In Ecclesiastes 4, Solomon presents four problems he has observed on the earth: oppression, rivalry, loneliness, and the government. Through these observations, Solomon teaches us further how worldly gain and power are pursuits of the wind.

Solomon begins by discussing the problem of oppression. He describes how he has observed the tears of the oppressed and how those who are supposed to help the oppressed do not. This reality causes Solomon to say it is better for those who are dead than those who are not yet born, for they do not have to experience the current wickedness of this world.

Solomon next observes the problem of rivalry. Solomon has continually made comments and opinions about labor, and in this observation, Solomon sees how those who work hard do so out of rivalry. Instead of doing their work with a vision for the common good, they work to compete with others. In our world today, we can see how this is a sad reality. While there are businesses and organizations that link arms with others, there are many other corpo-

> We can live in the present with purpose and hope as we fix our eyes on eternity.

rations that thrive on competition. These places desire to be the ones on top and can even go about their work in manipulative ways to accomplish this desire.

Solomon also includes a proverb that describes how a foolish person is lazy about their work. Their laziness has consequences, as their lack of work contributes to starvation for themselves. Yet Solomon claims it is better to have some rest in this life than to work hard for no eternal gain. Verses 5 and 6 may appear to contradict one another, but they reveal the perspective Solomon has been taking thus far. If this world is all there is, then one might have some laxity when it comes to their work.

In verses 7–8, Solomon observes the problem of loneliness. He describes how there are people who do not have a friend, child, or sibling. Their lack of companionship possibly leads them to seek comfort and satisfaction in riches. Yet, even still, they are not content. Without anyone to work for, they feel as if there is no purpose to their work. In comparison to loneliness, Solomon describes the importance of community in verses 9–11. He teaches how there are benefits in community that one in isolation does not receive. Those with a community have someone to help them, comfort them, and fight with them. The one in isolation, however, is left without aid, comfort, and defense. Solomon includes a popular proverbial phrase in verse 12 that teaches how a cord of three strands is not easily broken. The increase of two to three in this verse reveals how there is power in numbers.

Verses 7–11 teach us the value of community. The lonely person presented turned to riches for their source of comfort and satisfaction, but they remained broken. This person reminds us how we should not place our identity in riches. Even if our riches are great, we can be without the companionship for which we were created. Genesis 2:18 says, "Then the Lord God said, 'It is not good for the man to be alone. I will make a helper corresponding to him.'" Mankind is designed to live in community. While family, relationships, and friendships should not be our ultimate source of identity or satisfaction, we need community to come alongside us and speak truth into our lives.

Lastly, Solomon observes the problem of the government. He explains that a poor but wise youth is better than an old and foolish king who refuses wisdom. These verses connect to the first problem presented and observed. Those in government authority who do not listen to wise counsel will make foolish decisions that affect the people in their country. Instead of caring for their people, they oppress them due to pride in their power. Solomon continues with this language of a youth and king in verses 14–16. These verses are hard to interpret, but they seem to describe how the poor youth rose to kingship after being in prison.

If this youth is the same as the one mentioned in verse 13, then he likely ruled in wisdom. Yet the people did not rejoice in him as king. These verses reveal how even if someone rules with wisdom, it is not promised that the people under their leadership will listen and respect them.

As we look at our own world today, we can see how these problems of oppression, rivalry, loneliness, and political turmoil are present. Solomon does not seem to offer any solutions to these problems, which can lead us to feel discouraged. But yet again, the open-endedness of these observations points us to our need for Jesus. Without Jesus, there is no hope for oppression, rivalry, loneliness, and political turmoil. Sinful mankind cannot make this world better—only Jesus can. It is the grace and forgiveness of Christ that brings healing to the broken places of this world.

Those who come to faith in Jesus are empowered to share the hope of the gospel with those who are oppressed. As believers, we are given a spirit of camaraderie instead of competition. Through the gift of the Church, we receive a life-giving community that reveals the power of numbers. By the Spirit, we receive wisdom on how to engage with political matters.

While the world we live in remains tainted by sin, we do not despair. The brokenness we see and experience compels us to view our world through the lens of the gospel. It is only when we observe our world through the lens of the gospel that we see everything clearly. This life is not all there is, so we can live in the present with purpose and hope as we fix our eyes on eternity.

study questions

What key words or themes stood out to you from reading Ecclesiastes?

_____

_____

_____

_____

_____

study questions

Read the passages in the second column, and write in the third column what these passages compel us to do, as believers, about the four problems Solomon observed.

Oppression	Proverbs 14:21	
Rivalry	Philippians 2:2–3	
Loneliness	Galatians 6:2	
Political Turmoil	1 Peter 2:13–17	

How should the four problems Solomon presents (oppression, rivalry, loneliness, political turmoil) move us to place our hope in Jesus?

_____
_____
_____
_____
_____
_____
_____
_____
_____
_____

Notes

When approaching God in prayer and reading His Word, we must come with a heart to listen and obey.

week two day two

Fear God

READ ECCLESIASTES 5:1–7

Suppose a traveler to the Holy Land of Israel wants to visit a historic church, but a service is taking place at the time. In that case, the visitor may still be allowed to enter during the service but be told that no photography is permitted and be encouraged to be silent. Being in an ancient church while these services are happening is a remarkable experience. The sound of singing echoes off the walls, and the light entering through the stained glass windows makes the experience awe-inspiring. That feeling and sense of awe are what we all ought to experience when we enter into worship with God. This idea of reverence and proper worship is what Solomon teaches in these seven verses. Solomon breaks away from making observations to teaching about the importance of approaching God rightly and living in fear of the Lord.

Solomon begins by encouraging his readers to guard their steps when they go to the house of God. At this time, the house of God was the temple. Solomon followed through with his father's plans and built a temple as Israel's place of worship. The temple was where God's presence would come to dwell, and it was the place where sacrifices would be held so that the Israelites could be cleansed from their sin. Not treating the temple with reverence would

> The quest for meaning, satisfaction, and purpose is fulfilled in fear of the Lord.

be dishonoring to God, which is why Solomon warns to watch how one approaches the temple. He teaches how it is better to approach worship with obedience than to worship God with a dishonoring heart. To offer sacrifices as fools do would be to offer a sacrifice with a heart that does not seek to obey the Lord. Solomon's words reflect what Jesus spoke to the Pharisees when He revealed their empty worship. Jesus says in Mark 7:6–7, "This people honors me with their lips, but their heart is far from me. They worship me in vain, teaching as doctrines human commands."

Solomon goes on to teach about reverent prayer. Temple sacrifices in Scripture were typically offered in silence. After sacrifices were given, there would be a reading of the Law, and then the people would respond either in a prayer, song, or personal vow to God. Just like approaching the temple sacrifice with reverence, so does Solomon give the command to approach God's Word with reverence. To interrupt the reading of the Law would reveal a heart that did not desire to listen to God's Word. It would be like a visitor to the Holy Land interrupting the church service instead of being silent. Just as the Israelites were to approach this time before the Lord with reverence, so should we. When approaching God in prayer and reading His Word, we must come with a heart to listen and obey.

Solomon reminds his readers how God is in heaven, and they are on earth. In other words, remember that you are speaking to a God who is holy, righteous, and seated on the throne. If someone were to approach the king, they would be intentional with the words they speak, not hasty or irreverent. In the same way, when we pray, we should approach God with a posture of respect.

Connected to irreverent prayers are unfulfilled vows. Solomon teaches in verse 4 not to delay when fulfilling a vow to the Lord. Often, when someone would go to the temple, they would make a vow to God. These vows would involve making a request from God with the promise to do something for Him if He fulfills their request. It is possible to make a vow to God with a worshipful heart, but it is also possible to make a vow to God with an irreverent heart.

For example, some of us may know someone who has promised to go to church if God would work in their lives in a certain way. But once they get out of their trouble, they might just say a word of thanks to God only to go back to living their normal lives apart from Him. Solomon warns that it is better not to make a vow than to make a vow you fail to fulfill. Failing to fulfill a vow to God reveals a heart that does not genuinely want to obey the Lord. This person only wanted to get something from God without the intention of giving God what they promised.

Solomon ends these verses of caution with the words "fear God" (verse 7). To avoid falling into irreverent worship habits, we must fear the Lord. But what does it mean to fear the Lord? To fear the Lord is to obey Him, delight in Him, and approach Him with awe and reverence. When we fear the Lord, we worship Him rightly. We will not approach God with the wrong intentions or words of empty praise. Instead, we will honor God as we seek to obey His Word and glorify Him.

Solomon explains the importance of fearing the Lord when he writes in Proverbs 1:7, "The fear of the Lord is the beginning of knowledge." True wisdom involves fearing the Lord. Solomon will speak further about the fear of the Lord, but the inclusion of this teaching here hints at what Ecclesiastes is all about. The quest for meaning, satisfaction, and purpose is fulfilled in fear of the Lord.

The ability to fear the Lord would not be possible without Jesus. Because of our sinful nature, we fail to worship God as we should. But when we trust in Jesus, we are forgiven of our misplaced worship. The grace of Jesus gives us access to God and the ability to worship Him rightly. With the help of the Holy Spirit, we are able to worship God consistently and walk in obedience to Him. As believers, we are in a relationship with the God on high who has come near us. May this truth prompt us to approach Him in awe, delight, and humble submission.

study questions

In what ways do you fail to worship God as you should? Confess these areas to the Lord in prayer.

study questions

Read Romans 12:1. According to this verse, how are we to live as believers? What does this look like?

How can you fear God on a daily basis? List three practical ways you can fear God this week.

Notes

The Spirit aids us in keeping Jesus as the King of our lives and serving Him alone.

week two day three

The Futility of Wealth

READ ECCLESIASTES 5:8–6:9

Solomon has been speaking about the futility of wealth throughout Ecclesiastes, and in today's passage, he speaks about this theme again. In chapter 4, we learned how wealth does not solve the problem of loneliness. Through today's passage, Solomon teaches how wealth does not bring satisfaction. Instead, Solomon reminds his readers it is far greater to be content with what someone has than ruin their life in pursuit of gain.

Solomon begins with a quick note about injustice. He describes how injustice should be no surprise because the government is corrupt. Instead of protecting and giving to the poor, those in leadership often look out for themselves and take for themselves. The greediness of these leaders connects with Solomon's following thoughts about wealth.

Solomon teaches in Ecclesiastes 5:10 how those who love silver and wealth are ultimately not satisfied with what they have. Even if someone's riches increase, their expenses and responsibilities often increase as well. We can relate to this problem in our day, as it seems more money is always needed to pay our bills, stock our fridges, and cover additional expenses. The reality of having much but still needing to spend causes the rich to be restless. Solomon also compares the one who spends with the

> Everything we have been given is a gift from God. In Christ, our Giver, we have all we need.

one who hoards. Solomon describes a situation in Ecclesiastes 5:14–15 in which a man hoarded his money only to lose it in a bad venture. His foolish decision caused him to be empty-handed and unable to provide for his children.

Solomon reminds us of the reality of our possessions and riches in Ecclesiastes 5:15. We came into this world naked and possessing nothing, and we will leave this world in the same way. Solomon describes this reality as a "sickening tragedy" (Ecclesiastes 5:16). The one who pursues riches and money ultimately gains nothing. Instead of experiencing joy and the blessings of community, he is alone, frustrated, and sick.

After comparing people who spend and hoard, Solomon offers a glimmer of hope by comparing the rich who spend and hoard to the person who enjoys what they have. In Ecclesiastes 5:18, Solomon reminds his readers for a third time that it is good to eat, drink, and enjoy one's labor. Just like the other instances of this idea, Solomon connects this statement with a truth about God. He says that it is God who has given each person the days of his life, as well as riches and wealth. Those who have received wealth from God can view what they have been given as a gift. This positive perspective about wealth reveals how having money is not in and of itself a bad thing. In His kindness, God bestows money to people as a gift. However, while money is a gift, mankind is not to place their identity and security in this gift and should be ready and willing to use that blessing to help others.

That is why Solomon teaches in Ecclesiastes 6:2 how God has given people riches and wealth, but He does not allow people to enjoy them. On the surface, this may seem like a contradiction to Solomon's previous thoughts. Yet these words reveal how there are limitations God has placed on the gift of wealth. Money and riches are not our ultimate means for satisfaction—God is. Solomon's grief over the inability to enjoy wealth causes him to say that a stillborn child is better off than the one with wealth because the child has rest. This is a sad illustration given by Solomon, but it reveals how the love of money is an empty pursuit. There is no rest for those who place their value and security in money alone.

Even though Solomon is still sorting through his perspective of wealth, his thoughts about viewing wealth as a gift have placed him on the right track. When we see that our possessions are a gift from God, we will not be as entitled or foolish with our money. Furthermore, when we seek to put the Giver first in our lives, we will not be tempted by the riches of this world. The Bible does not condemn having money, but it does warn about the love of money. The author of Hebrews illustrates this point when he writes, "Keep your life free from the love of money. Be satisfied with what you have, for he himself has said, I will never leave you or abandon you" (Hebrews 13:5). When we keep our lives free from the love of money, we are able to depend on the One who never forsakes us. Putting God first—delighting in and depending on Him—keeps our hearts content. The contentment that comes from the Lord allows us to enjoy what we have been given instead of exploiting what we have been given.

The desire for wealth and riches can be a hard desire to fight against in our world today. In our own lives, we will battle against the craving to have much and struggle with placing our security in what we have. Thankfully, we are not alone in this fight against our flesh. Through the power of the Holy Spirit, given to us in Christ, we have the strength to resist indulging in wealth. The Spirit aids us in keeping Jesus as the King of our lives and serving Him alone. The Holy Spirit also gives us wisdom on how to use our money wisely and prompts us to give rather than take. In the moments we find ourselves placing our security in what we have, may we remember how everything we have been given is a gift from God. In Christ, our Giver, we have all we need.

study questions

Read 1 Timothy 6:6–10. What does it look like to have godliness with contentment? How does being content with our basic necessities keep us from pursuing the love of money?

_____

_____

_____

_____

_____

study questions

How can you enjoy what God has given you without placing your security and ultimate joy in what you have been given?

_____
_____
_____
_____
_____
_____
_____
_____
_____

Scripture tells us that putting anything before God is idolatry (Deuteronomy 5:6–7). Why is worshiping God first important as believers?

_____
_____
_____
_____
_____
_____
_____
_____
_____

Notes

Instead of fighting against God's sovereignty, we can rest in God's sovereignty.

week two day four

Consider the Work of God

READ ECCLESIASTES 6:10–7:14

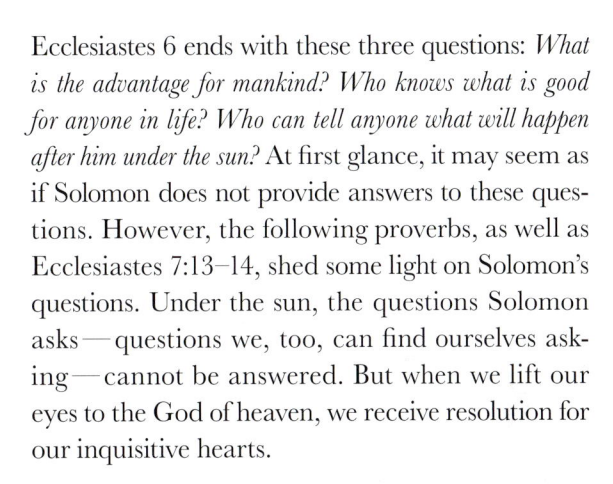

Ecclesiastes 6 ends with these three questions: *What is the advantage for mankind? Who knows what is good for anyone in life? Who can tell anyone what will happen after him under the sun?* At first glance, it may seem as if Solomon does not provide answers to these questions. However, the following proverbs, as well as Ecclesiastes 7:13–14, shed some light on Solomon's questions. Under the sun, the questions Solomon asks—questions we, too, can find ourselves asking—cannot be answered. But when we lift our eyes to the God of heaven, we receive resolution for our inquisitive hearts.

Chapter 7 of Ecclesiastes is written in a similar style to the book of Proverbs. In fact, these verses even reflect the teachings we see in Proverbs. Solomon employs his "better to" or "better than" language to give wisdom on how one should live. In verse 1, Solomon teaches that it is better to have a good reputation than to possess fine perfume. Similarly, Proverbs 22:1 says, "A good name is to be chosen over great wealth; favor is better than silver and gold." These words teach how it is far greater to be known for being someone who did what was right than one who chased momentary pleasures.

In Ecclesiastes 7:1b–4, Solomon encourages a realistic perspective about death. Solomon teaches in

> When we consider the works of God, we are given a proper perspective on eternity.

Ecclesiastes 7:2 that it is better to go to a house of mourning than a house of feasting since death is the end of all mankind. He encourages those who are living to take the reality of death to heart rather than ignore it. In Ecclesiastes 7:4, we read how the heart of the wise is in the house of mourning, whereas the heart of the fool is in the house of pleasure. Solomon uses language of "the heart" to describe what drives us. The heart of the wise is driven by understanding and accepting grief, but pleasure and laughter drive the heart of the fool.

These verses could appear to contradict Solomon's previous words about how we should eat, drink, and enjoy life in the present. However, those previous lessons do not become void because of Solomon's words in these verses. Rather, both of the ideas are held in tension. Laughter and feasting are not in and of themselves bad. However, the fools are those who laugh and feast with no thought to eternity. It is foolish to ignore the reality of death and live as if one will not face death. But the wise are those who accept the reality of death and allow it to impact how they live in the present.

Solomon continues to compare and contrast the fool and the wise in Ecclesiastes 7:5–7. He teaches how it is better to listen to a wise rebuke than the song of fools or meaningless words. This teaching about rebuke reflects multiple passages in Proverbs that speak about the importance of discipline (Proverbs 10:17, 12:1, 13:1). Even though receiving a rebuke or discipline can be hard, correction is for our good. We can look at our own lives and see how God has used His Word and other people to shape us through words of correction. Receiving and listening to rebuke helps us grow, but listening to the songs of fools hinders our growth.

In Ecclesiastes 7:8–10, Solomon teaches how to approach time and one's attitude with wisdom. Solomon explains that it is better to have a patient spirit than an angry or proud spirit. He also warns not to dwell on the past or to look at the present with disdain. Living with a discontent heart that compares the present with the past is not wise.

Solomon concludes these proverbs with an exhortation to consider the work of God. Similarly, in Ecclesiastes 7:14, Solomon says to consider the fact that God has appointed both the day of prosperity and the day of adversity. We can long to straighten out what seems unfair or frustrating and to know with certainty what lies beyond death, but without considering the work of God, our longings will not be met. Ecclesiastes 6:10 says that mankind "is not able to contend with the one stronger than he." What Solomon is teaching us in Ecclesiastes 7:13–14 is that instead of fighting against God's sovereignty, we can rest in God's sovereignty.

When we consider God's sovereignty, we can view both days of joy and adversity with the right perspective. Our sovereign God grants us both happy and hard days for our good. When we consider the works of God and rest in His sovereignty, we are reminded of how to live. We are reminded that we can live with open hands and trust God no matter our circumstances. We are reminded how God has turned hard and evil things, like His own Son's crucifixion, into good.

Therefore, the questions we started with—"Who knows what is good for anyone in life?" and "Who can tell anyone what will happen after him under the sun?"—find their answers in Ecclesiastes 7:13–14. It is God who knows what is good for our lives and tells us what happens after we die. And what is the advantage for mankind? To consider the works of God and allow His works to guide us in wisdom.

When we consider the works of God, we are given a proper perspective of eternity. God's Word tells us how God's sovereign plan of redemption, accomplished through Jesus Christ, saves us from the punishment of our sin and grants us eternal life. As believers, our lives are lived through the lens of the gospel with eternity in mind. Unlike those who ignore death, as believers, we live in hope in the face of death. Unlike those who ignore eternity, we live in light of eternity. An eternal perspective allows us to enjoy life in the present while also looking with joy to the future.

study questions

How are you prone to fight against God's sovereignty instead of resting in God's sovereignty? How can considering God's works help you rest in Him?

study questions

How does being realistic about death and aware of what lies beyond death help us to live in the present with wisdom?

_____
_____
_____
_____
_____
_____
_____
_____
_____
_____

Read 1 Thessalonians 4:13. This verse reminds us that Christians grieve differently than the world because we have hope. Where do we find our hope?

_____
_____
_____
_____
_____
_____
_____
_____
_____
_____
_____
_____
_____

Notes

Even though the world is stained by sin, there is redemption found in Jesus Christ.

week two day five

The Stain of Sin

READ ECCLESIASTES 7:15–29

At times, it can seem as though unbelievers have it easy. We can look at the news and see how convicted criminals are set free even though the evidence proves they have done wrong. We know of evil people who live long and happy lives, while others experience suffering after suffering. The reality of brokenness and sin is what Solomon observes in today's passage. Through his observations, we learn how even though the world is stained by sin, there is redemption found in Jesus Christ.

Solomon starts by observing how the unrighteous often seem to live long, but the righteous do not. This observation from Solomon is a generalization more than a proven fact, but we can understand his opinion. Often, it can seem as if those who are "good" suffer more than those who are "bad." We hear stories about good people who are killed in an accident or lose their babies too soon, and we can feel as if the world is unfair.

Solomon goes on to teach not to be excessively righteous or wise (verse 16). This statement from Solomon could cause us to balk. His words appear to contradict multiple passages of Scripture that encourage and even command us to pursue wisdom and righteousness. But the words "excessively" and "overly" provide further insight. Solomon is teach-

> The stain of sin is washed away with Jesus's blood.

ing how it is possible to take righteousness and wisdom so far that it makes one prideful.

We can think of the Pharisees in the New Testament, who boasted of their righteousness and their knowledge of the Scriptures. Yet their boasting and legalism demonstrated how they were more focused on upholding a holy image than on having a holy heart. In the same way, we too can find ourselves being excessively righteous or overly wise when we care more about pursuing holiness for the sake of favor with God rather than obedience to God.

Contrasted with not being excessively righteous and overly wise is the warning not to be excessively wicked and foolish. Solomon includes the question, "Why should you die before your time?" (verse 17) to teach how being excessively wicked and foolish could lead to a life cut short. Modern examples can include when someone dies from being reckless or when a mob leader is killed by an enemy.

Solomon explains how grasping both the realities of righteousness and sinfulness is good. He includes how the one who fears the Lord will end up with both of them, or as other translations say, "avoid all extremes" (verse 18, NIV). Those who fear the Lord and walk in His wisdom will avoid the extremes of lawlessness and legalism.

Solomon then teaches about the reality of sinful mankind. He describes how wisdom makes the wise stronger than multiple powerful rulers. Yet, even if someone is wise, there is no person on this earth who is truly righteous and never sins. If we glance down to verse 29, we see how Solomon expands on this idea further. He describes how in his quest, he discovered how God made people upright, but they pursued many schemes. Here, Solomon's words connect back to Genesis 1–3. God created humans without sin and to live in obedience to Him. However, the first humans, Adam and Eve, chose to disregard God's commands and pursue their own schemes for control, wisdom, and satisfaction. Sadly, sin entered the world because of their disobedience, and all mankind is sinful because of them.

The disobedience of Adam and Eve is the reason for the brokenness of our world. Sin is the reason why there is suffering and death and why there are people who are wicked. Solomon describes wickedness in verse 26. He describes how, in his pursuit of understanding and knowledge, he found that a sinful woman leads others to destruction. The woman in these verses connects with the woman referenced in Proverbs, who is called "the woman Folly" (Proverbs 9:13, ESV). Woman Folly represents wickedness and is the opposite of Lady Wisdom, who represents righteousness. Those who allow themselves to be caught up in wickedness will be led to ruin. However, Solomon brings hope in light of wickedness at the end of verse 26. Those who obey and follow God will be rescued from sin.

We know these words to be true because of Jesus Christ. When we open up the pages of the New Testament, we learn how God came in the flesh to rescue mankind from their sin. Jesus died a death that we deserve for our sin and covers our unrighteous with His perfect righteousness. Paul, the author of the book of Romans, explains this clearly when he writes, "For while we were still helpless, at the right time, Christ died for the ungodly. For rarely will someone die for a just person—though for a good person, perhaps someone might even dare to die. But God proves his own love for us in that while we were still sinners, Christ died for us" (Romans 5:6–8). The stain of sin is washed away with Jesus's blood.

Because of Jesus, we are able to be people of righteousness. We can live in a world full of sin with hope rather than despair, knowing that Jesus has made us new, and one day He will make all things new. Although we will still struggle against our sin, Christ's grace, through the Spirit, empowers us to walk in righteousness. And even in the moments we feel as if the wicked win and the righteous suffer, we can remember how eternity with Jesus is the inheritance of every believer. Until the day we are united with our Savior, we walk in obedience to Him and rest in His righteousness.

study questions

How does the hope of the gospel bring comfort when suffering comes or injustice occurs?

_____
_____
_____
_____
_____
_____

study questions

What does it say about God's character that He is the One who rescues us from sin and makes us righteous?

_____
_____
_____
_____
_____
_____
_____
_____
_____
_____

Read Romans 6:13. What does it practically look like to be weapons for righteousness?

_____
_____
_____
_____
_____
_____
_____
_____
_____
_____
_____
_____

Notes

Scripture Memory

week two day six

Consider the work of God, for who can straighten out what he has made crooked? In the day of prosperity be joyful, but in the day of adversity, consider: God has made the one as well as the other.

ECCLESIASTES 7:13–14A

Week Two *Reflection*

Summarize the main points from this week's passages.

_____
_____
_____
_____

What did you observe from this week's text about God and His character?

_____
_____
_____
_____

What did these passages teach you about the condition of mankind and yourself?

_____
_____
_____
_____

READ ECCLESIASTES 4–7:29

How did these passages point to the gospel?

_____
_____
_____
_____

How should you respond to these passages?
What specific action steps can you take this week to apply them in your life?

_____
_____
_____
_____

Write a prayer in response to your study of God's Word. Adore God for who He is, confess sins He revealed in your own life, ask Him to empower you to walk in obedience, and pray for anyone who comes to mind as you study.

_____
_____
_____
_____
_____
_____

Where human leaders fall short in their authority reveals the ultimate authority of God.

week three day one

All Will Go Well

READ ECCLESIASTES 8:1–15

Have you ever watched a little kid defy authority? If you are a parent, maybe you have seen your child stomp their foot and refuse to listen to you. Or, if you are a teacher, maybe you have witnessed a student ignore your command. Humans are not always naturally inclined to submit to authority. We like to be the ones who are in control. But how are we, as believers, supposed to treat authority, especially if the person in authority is corrupt? Solomon explores these thoughts on authority in today's passage and gives believers hope in light of injustice.

Solomon encourages his readers to listen to those who are in authority. His reason for this exhortation is because of one's oath made before God. While this could mean either an oath made to the king in the presence of God or an oath made to God directly, we learn how obedience to God is what matters when it comes to listening to authority. Solomon also warns his readers to be respectful to the king when in his presence and not cause trouble. Those who submit to, rather than defy, authority will be kept from harm. We might read these verses and think Solomon is teaching us to submit to authority no matter the circumstances. But the verses that follow help expand on Solomon's words. In verse 5, Solomon explains that

> Solomon is continually teaching how we can still live with joy even in a corrupt world where death is inevitable.

while it is important to submit to authority, the wise know the right time and procedure to not listen to authority.

What Solomon is saying in verse 5 is that if a leader commands citizens to act in a way that defies how Scripture calls us to live as believers, Christians should obey Scripture rather than that leader. Believers are given wisdom through their relationship with God, by the power of the Spirit, to recognize these instances and know how to respond according to God's Word.

In verses 7–8, Solomon goes on to teach how even those in high authority do not have ultimate control. He describes how no one has the authority to control the wind or death. His words reveal the limitations of human authority. Where human leaders fall short in their authority reveals the ultimate authority of God. God is the One who is in control of all things. Even when human leaders fail or make evil decisions, we can trust our God, who is ultimately in control. As Romans 13:1 says, "Let everyone submit to the governing authorities, since there is no authority except from God, and the authorities that exist are instituted by God."

Solomon then moves away from teaching about authority to observations about injustice. He describes how the wicked are praised even if they have done wrong and how punishment for evil acts is delayed. The delay of punishment for evil causes even more people to commit wrongdoing since no punishment is being executed. Solomon also describes in verse 14 how the righteous often suffer while the unrighteous live well. While Solomon mourns this injustice, he provides hope a couple of verses earlier in verse 12. Even though a sinner does much evil, it will go well for those who fear the Lord. Solomon likely understands the eternal benefits God-fearing people receive that are not given to the wicked. His words remind us how we can remain dedicated to and trust the Lord in moments when injustice reigns. The wicked may carry on with their schemes for now, but they face an eternity of punishment because of their unrepentant sin.

Solomon ends his musings on authority and injustice by reminding his readers to eat, drink, and enjoy the present. Again, Solomon's words do not promote a hedonistic view or the belief that the pursuit of pleasure should be one's ultimate goal in life. Solomon is continually teaching how we can still live with joy even in a corrupt world where death is inevitable. And this joy is only possible through a relationship with the Lord.

As believers, we can have joy walking in this broken world because we know God's plans. We know that God's Word tells us how those who believe and trust in Jesus receive eternal life with Christ. We know that God's authority will one day supersede man's authority. We know that Christ will return to right every wrong. Because of the gospel, all will ultimately go well for believers in Christ.

Knowing and clinging to these truths can help us remain joyful and trusting in the Lord. The world we live in is desperately broken, and it can be extremely difficult to live in this world as believers. Even still, we can live with present joy as we keep eternity in mind. One day, the King of kings will come and transform this world into a place of righteousness, peace, and rest. Until that day, we submit to authority as we trust in the ultimate authority of God, walk in wisdom, and live with joy.

> "We can live with present joy as we keep eternity in mind."

study questions

How do you respond to authority? How does knowing God has ultimate authority help you respond to human authority?

_____
_____
_____
_____
_____
_____
_____

study questions

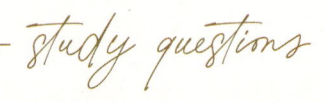

How does the gospel reveal the truth that it will go well for those who fear the Lord?

How does knowing it will go well for believers in the end shape the way you view the present?

Notes

The gift of eternal life causes us to live life with intentionality, faithfulness, and joy in the present.

week three day two

There is Hope

READ ECCLESIASTES 8:16–9:12

There is a once-popular song titled "Live Like You Were Dying." This song describes a man who receives an unfortunate diagnosis before the middle of his life. In response to his days being few, he decides to live his life to the fullest and do everything he was always too scared to try. The man in this song says these words to the singer, "Someday, I hope you get the chance to live like you were dying." While these lyrics may be catchy and easy to sing along to, the reality is each one of us is, in fact, headed toward death. Death is unavoidable and can happen at any time. In these passages, Solomon observes the reality of death again and encourages us to live like we are dying.

Before Solomon speaks about death, he describes the limits of wisdom in Ecclesiastes 8:16–17. He explains how he applied his mind to know wisdom and observed the activities that are done on the earth. However, in this quest of observation, Solomon concludes that no one is able to discover the meaning of the works done under the sun. Even those who are wise and seek to discover the truth of how the world works find themselves left without an answer. Solomon's words may seem hopeless on the surface, but they can be a great comfort. It is good to realize that what we see with our eyes cannot

There is hope for the reality of death — and it is found in Jesus Christ.

fully answer our hearts' longings or our minds' questions. This reality combats a popular view that we can gain truth from our experiences alone. Solomon reveals the fallacy of that argument: our experiences and observations cannot provide us with complete understanding. It is only when we lift our eyes from under the sun to gaze at the God of heaven that we can know the truth.

Solomon then moves into his observations about death. He starts with a word of comfort that "the righteous, the wise, and their works" are in the sovereign hands of God (Ecclesiastes 9:1). However, no matter if one is righteous or unrighteous — all will experience death. Solomon's descriptions of sacrifices and cleanliness reveal that even if one lives a good and morally upright life, one cannot escape death. Solomon also teaches in Ecclesiastes 9:3 how the hearts of mankind are full of evil. Solomon's words remind us of the fallen condition of all mankind. Because of the fall, every human heart is sinful. No matter how much we try to deny this truth, God's Word makes it clear that "the wages of sin is death" (Romans 6:23).

Solomon also describes how death can come suddenly (Ecclesiastes 9:11–12). The weak and the strong, the wise and the foolish, the rich and the poor cannot escape death. No one knows when their time of death will come, and all can find death suddenly falling upon them unexpectedly. Like many passages in Ecclesiastes, these observations from Solomon can leave us feeling downcast. However, Solomon speaks words of hope and encouragement even in light of the reality of death.

If we go back to Ecclesiastes 9:4, we read that Solomon teaches that there is hope for those who are with the living. This means that there is hope for those who understand the reality of death and live through the lens of the fleeting nature of life. As Solomon has taught previously, it does a person a disservice to ignore the reality of death. When one comes to terms with the reality of death, they can embrace the gift of life.

Solomon expands on this idea further in Ecclesiastes 9:7–10. Here, Solomon employs his sixth exhortation to eat, drink, and enjoy one's life. This time, however, Solomon provides specific examples of how to do this. He encourages his readers in Ecclesiastes 9:7–8 to eat bread, drink wine, let their clothes be white, and never let oil be lacking on their heads. Food, clothing, and oil were all considered necessities in ancient Israel. Therefore, Solomon instructs us to enjoy the necessities of life that we have received. Solomon also encourages his readers to enjoy life with their spouses (Ecclesiastes 9:9). Since this life is fleeting, and marriage does not remain beyond the grave (Matthew 22:30), one can embrace the time they have been given with their spouse. The last thing we will discuss in this passage is how Solomon encourages hard work (Ecclesiastes 9:10). Solomon exhorts that whatever work one does should be done with all of their strength.

The ability to work hard and enjoy the gifts of life connects with this teaching in Ecclesiastes 9:7, which reads, "for God has already accepted your works." Solomon lived many centuries before the Apostle Paul would teach about justification by faith, yet Solomon's words reveal a basic understanding of this doctrine. One can enjoy life in the present, even with the reality of death, because they have received God's approval. This approval is not achieved by one's works but by the grace of God. Through the sacrifice of Jesus, we are forgiven for our sins and approved in God's eyes.

The approval we receive from Jesus grants us eternal life with Him. The wages of sin may be death, "but the gift of God is eternal life in Christ Jesus our Lord" (Romans 6:23). The burden of death is released for believers in Christ. Even though death will still come to us all, the hope we possess as believers is that we will be raised to eternal life with Christ. The gift of eternal life causes us to live life with intentionality, faithfulness, and joy in the present. Unlike others who "live it up," thinking death is the end, as believers, we are able to truly live, knowing death is not the end. Though death is serious, sad, and often sudden, our joy as believers can point others to the life available through Christ. There is hope for the reality of death—and it is found in Jesus Christ.

study questions

Read 1 Corinthians 10:31 and Colossians 3:23–24. How can you glorify God with your work and the good gifts He has given you?

_____

_____

_____

_____

_____

_____

study questions

How does our approval in Christ fuel your joy?

How can your perspective on death as a believer point others to the good news of the gospel?

Notes

The attitude of Christ teaches us how a posture of peace is greater than a posture of pride.

week three day three

The Benefits of Wisdom

READ ECCLESIASTES 9:13–10:20

Throughout Ecclesiastes, Solomon has discussed the themes of wisdom, folly, injustice, and corrupt government. In today's passage, Solomon speaks to all of these ideas. However, the organization of these themes in this passage is notably haphazard. And even though Solomon's line of thought is not exactly linear, we can still learn from his teachings. Through these verses, we learn three benefits of wisdom: an attitude of peace, discernment, and wise leadership.

First, Solomon teaches us about an attitude of peace. In Ecclesiastes 9:17, Solomon compares the words of the wise to the words of a loud ruler. The wise possess calm words, and their words are heeded more than the shouts of a ruler. Similarly, in Ecclesiastes 10:4, Solomon describes how choosing to be calm instead of angry puts great offenses to rest. Solomon teaches in Ecclesiastes 10:12 how the words of a wise person are gracious. In comparison, the words of the fool consume him, and his speech consists of evil madness. Solomon also warns his readers in Ecclesiastes 10:20 to refrain from speaking ill against those in leadership, even in private.

Solomon's teachings about an attitude of peace reflect the attitude of Christ. Throughout Jesus's ministry, He maintained a posture of calmness even

> As believers, we can live differently as we obey and reflect our God of Wisdom.

when others opposed Him or tried to test Him. When Jesus was betrayed, He did not resist or speak out against those arresting Him. Even when He stood on trial, "He did not commit sin, and no deceit was found in his mouth; when he was insulted, he did not insult in return; when he suffered, he did not threaten but entrusted himself to the one who judges justly" (1 Peter 2:22–23). The attitude of Christ teaches us how a posture of peace is greater than a posture of pride.

Next, Solomon teaches about discernment. In Ecclesiastes 10:2, Solomon describes how the wise person's heart goes to the right, whereas the fool's heart goes to the left. The "right" in Scripture refers to the way that leads to righteousness, while the "left" refers to the way of unrighteousness. The unwise have a heart that lacks sense, and their actions prove to others their foolishness (Ecclesiastes 10:3). Ecclesiastes 10:8–11 likely describes the actions of the unwise. While a wise person could also perform these actions, these verses most likely describe the consequences of a foolish person's actions. Ecclesiastes 10:10 suggests this, as Solomon teaches how the advantage of wisdom is that it brings success. For the fool, however, their lack of discernment and laziness can lead them to become hurt or cause them to overwork themselves.

Lastly, Solomon describes wise leadership. He tells a story in Ecclesiastes 9:14 about a small city that was besieged by a great king. A poor wise man delivered the city with his wisdom. Yet, after the city's deliverance, the man was soon forgotten. In Ecclesiastes 10:17, Solomon teaches how a land is blessed when those in leadership possess self-control and enjoy pleasures with an attitude of wisdom instead of foolishness. However, Solomon includes how this world's brokenness causes leadership to be skewed. Earlier, in Ecclesiastes 10:6–7, Solomon describes how he has seen the fool appointed to great leadership, whereas the rich remain in lowly positions. Solomon likely uses the word "rich" instead of "poor" here to teach how those who possess resources do not always get placed in high authority while those who do not have as many resources get appointed. Solomon also teaches how although it is better to lead with wisdom, this world does not always consistently honor or favor wisdom.

Solomon's teachings yet again reflect Jesus. Jesus is the epitome of a wise leader. Centuries before Jesus's birth, the prophet Isaiah foretold how Jesus would be a Wonderful Counselor and a Prince of Peace who would rule over God's kingdom with justice and righteousness forever (Isaiah 9). Unlike a corrupt or unwise king, Jesus is the perfect King who reigns with flawless wisdom and righteousness. Because Jesus is God, His wisdom has no limits, and His actions are always just and right. Yet even though Jesus is our perfect and wise King, He was not treated as such during His earthly ministry. Jesus's wisdom was often rejected by others, and He was mocked for claiming to be King.

People may have disregarded Jesus as King, but Christ's triumph over sin and death through His crucifixion and resurrection reveals His ultimate kingship. Through His sacrifice, Jesus delivered mankind from the punishment of death, and He allows all who trust in Him to enter into God's kingdom. Therefore, Jesus is the fulfillment of the poor wise man in this passage, who delivers not just a city but the whole world through His wisdom.

This world may be skewed in terms of what is seen as wise leadership, but because of Jesus, we hope in the One who reigns over all. Not only this, but as believers, we receive the benefits of wisdom through our relationship with Christ. In a world filled with people who are hasty with their speech and speak words that put down others, by the power of the Spirit, we are able to control our tongues and speak words that build up rather than tear down.

Unlike those who disregard obedience to God and pursue their own means for wisdom, as followers of Christ, we walk in the wisdom of God's Word and follow the One "who became wisdom from God for us" (1 Corinthians 1:30). Although we live in a world that follows foolishness rather than the wisdom of God, as believers, we can live differently as we obey and reflect our God of wisdom.

study questions

Read Ecclesiastes 10:4 and Proverbs 22:11. How can a peaceful attitude in comparison to an opposing attitude impact those in higher authority?

_____

_____

_____

_____

_____

study questions

Read James 1:5. Where does wisdom come from, and how is it received? How does this verse encourage you in your own life?

_____
_____
_____
_____
_____
_____
_____
_____
_____

How can you choose to continuously walk in wisdom, even in a world that embraces foolishness more than the wisdom of God?

_____
_____
_____
_____
_____
_____
_____
_____
_____
_____

Notes

As believers, we walk toward our Creator with confidence and joy because we have been forgiven.

week three day four

Remember Your Creator

READ ECCLESIASTES 11–12:8

As Ecclesiastes comes to a close, Solomon takes some time to once again speak on the topic of death. Solomon's repetitive teaching on this theme reveals the seriousness of considering the reality of death and how to live life in light of death. Solomon also applies his final "everything is futile" statement to remind his readers of the fleeting nature of life. Death is inevitable, and this world is fleeting, so let us not waste the life we have been given.

In chapter 11, Solomon lists four ways to live in light of our Creator. The first is to work for our Creator. In Ecclesiastes 11:1–6, Solomon warns against slothfulness and emphasizes the importance of working hard. The person in Ecclesiastes 11:4 who watches the weather reflects those of us who put off our work until the conditions are favorable. Solomon commands us to get up and work hard no matter the circumstances. These verses remind us how our work is important and has a purpose (Colossians 3:23–24). Just as Adam worked the garden out of joyful service to the Lord, so are we to joyfully take up the work God has given us to serve Him.

Additionally, in Ecclesiastes 11:1–2, Solomon teaches about sharing one's provision with others. The provision God gifts us through our work is not to be kept to ourselves but shared with others. This prin-

Will we let our days pass us by? Or will we remember our Creator and live for Him?

ciple reflects the command of God to "love your neighbor as yourself" (Leviticus 19:18). As we work heartily and happily for the Lord, we are to open our hands to share the fruits of our labor. In doing so, we reflect the sacrifice of Jesus, who gave Himself up for us so we could receive salvation and eternal life.

Next, Solomon calls us to trust in our Creator. In Ecclesiastes 11:5–6, Solomon explains how we do not know the future and cannot know the work of God, who makes everything. As we have learned before in Ecclesiastes, God's sovereignty leads us to trust God. Instead of being frustrated that we cannot fully understand the mysteries of God, we can trust in the sovereignty of God.

Solomon also encourages us to rejoice in what our Creator has given us. In Ecclesiastes 11:7–10, Solomon teaches how we should rejoice in our lives while we remain living. Both the young person and the one who has lived many years should rejoice that they have been given these days to live. Solomon continues the theme of joy by encouraging readers to walk in the ways of their hearts and the desire of their eyes and remove sorrow and sin from their hearts. These verses remind us of Solomon's previous statements to enjoy life because it is a gift from God. We can respond to the life and gifts from God we have received with joy and gratitude.

This leads us to our last exhortation: to walk toward our Creator with confidence and joy.

One day, we will all stand before God to receive judgment for our works (Ecclesiastes 11:9). However, those in Christ do not have to fear this day. Because of the forgiveness of Christ, we will be declared guiltless on the day of judgment. As believers, we walk toward our Creator with confidence and joy because we have been forgiven.

In chapter 12, Solomon speaks about the reality of growing old. He uses figurative language to describe what it is like for a person who is close to death. The trembling of the house and the stooped men in Ecclesiastes 12:3 likely reflect the weakness of one's body. Similarly, seeing dimly through the windows in Ecclesiastes 12:3 likely symbolizes weakened eyesight. In Ecclesiastes 12:4, the shut doors and the fading sound of the mill likely reflect poor hearing. Whether we would like to admit it, this is the reality for each one of us. Our sharp senses will fade, and our strength will weaken. Many seek to resist aging, but even the most powerful products cannot fully stop the process of aging. We will grow old and lose the vitality of youth we currently possess. In Ecclesiastes 12:5–7, Solomon describes the brevity of one's life. One day, our lives will end, we will head to our eternal home, and our spirits will return to God—either to be with Him or to be sent away from Him.

Throughout chapter 12, Solomon repeats the word "before." With this word, Solomon teaches how there is a way to live before old age and death become a reality. What must one do before this time? The beginning of chapter 12 tells us to remember our Creator in the days of our youth. Here, we see how Solomon's wisdom in chapter 11 connects to the command of Ecclesiastes 12:1. Instead of wasting away our youth, pretending as if old age and death will not come to us, we ought to remember our Creator. We ought to remember who made us and that He has given us life.

The command to "remember your Creator" also has eternal implications. If one chooses to reject the forgiveness of Christ and forget their Creator, they may stand before Him one day guilty because of their disobedience and unrepentance. But those who accept the gift of Christ and remember their Creator will live for their Creator. For us who believe, we will remember the God who created us, saved us, and sustains us. Knowing that we will be united one day with our Creator encourages us to take up the life He has given us with joy, serve Him, and obey Him.

Solomon ends today's passage with these words: "'Absolute futility,' says the Teacher. 'Everything is futile'" (Ecclesiastes 12:8). Here, the word "futility" means "fleeting." Everything in this world is fleeting, including our lives, so how will we choose to live? Will we let our days pass us by? Or will we remember our Creator and live for Him?

study questions

The word "pain" in Ecclesiastes 11:10 means "evil." How is remembering our Creator and the fleeting nature of life connected to putting away evil and sin from our lives?

study questions

How do God's future judgment and the assurance of our salvation in Christ affect how we walk in the ways of our hearts and the desire of our eyes?

_____
_____
_____
_____
_____
_____
_____
_____
_____

Consider the four exhortations Solomon presents (work for your Creator, trust your Creator, rejoice in your Creator, and walk toward your Creator with confidence and joy). How can you practically respond to these exhortations in your everyday life?

_____
_____
_____
_____
_____
_____
_____
_____
_____
_____

Notes

Apart from God and His Word, we cannot receive true wisdom and understanding.

week three day five

The Conclusion of the Matter

READ ECCLESIASTES 12:9–14

Solomon has taken us down the journey of his past. He has revealed how the paths of riches, pleasures, and possessions all lead to a dead end. He has pointed out signs along the way that warn of the reality of injustice, wickedness, and death. But what now? The main takeaway of Solomon's teachings has been hinted at during the telling of his quest. The conclusion of the matter, Solomon says, is this: fear the Lord and keep His commands. Solomon has blocked off all the other roads for us, and he has pointed us to the path that leads to life.

Scholars disagree if the conclusion to Ecclesiastes is from the words of an editor or Solomon himself speaking in the third person. While both are possible, we will continue with the view that an editor has been recording Solomon's teachings and observations, and these final conclusions are derivative of Solomon's words. The editor writes how the Teacher, Solomon, was a man who bestowed upon people much wisdom and truth. He describes all the sayings of the wise as cattle prods (verse 11). Cattle prods were long staffs with sharp nails embedded in them. The shepherd in charge would use this staff to guide his animals in the right direction, away from harm.

> When the pursuits of this world leave us empty, we can turn to Jesus and be filled with His grace.

In the same way, wisdom gives us guidance in our lives and keeps us from wandering down paths that lead us to danger. The writer also says in verse 11 how wise sayings are like firmly embedded nails. That is, wisdom keeps us secure. The editor employs shepherding imagery again at the end of verse 11 by describing how wisdom is given by one Shepherd. Most Bible translators choose to capitalize the word "shepherd," believing the writer intended to speak about God. While human wisdom has its benefits, true wisdom comes from God. It is the wisdom of God that gives us direction, saves us from destruction, and keeps us secure.

In verse 12, the editor writes how it is unfruitful to continuously seek wisdom apart from God. He describes someone who hungrily consumes as much content as they can to receive wisdom. Yet the words "there is no end" and "wearies the body" reveal how the wisdom of this world cannot satisfy us. We can think of the shelves lined with self-help books in many bookstores and libraries—the fact that there are so many only points us to the limited nature of human wisdom and understanding. We do not need more self-help books; we only need the one book, the Bible, written by our wise Shepherd. Apart from God and His Word, we cannot receive true wisdom and understanding.

So then, what are we to do? We are to take all Solomon has taught us in Ecclesiastes and follow the path Solomon has led us to—the path of life. The path of life involves fearing the Lord and keeping His commands. Some of us may read these words and feel as if this path does not sound as fun as the other paths of pleasure and possessions. But Solomon has revealed to us the futility of passing pleasures, and he has taught us that to live in a futile world, we need to live by faith. When we walk the path of life and live by faith, we experience true satisfaction. The editor includes how God made each of us to worship and obey Him. Others may believe that living life on one's own terms is what brings satisfaction and joy. But when we submit our lives to the Lord and obey His commands, we live as the people we were created to be; we walk in the fullness of freedom and joy we were always meant to experience.

The editor reminds his readers to take the command to fear God and obey Him seriously because of God's future judgment. As we have already discussed, those of us who are in Christ do not need to fear this day. But those who ignore God's command to fear Him and obey Him should heed this warning. If you have dedicated your life to the path of riches and glory or the road of success, there is still time to turn around and pursue the path of life.

God has revealed the path of life to us in Christ. David presents this truth in Psalm 16:11 when he writes, "You reveal the path of life to me; in your presence is abundant joy; at your right hand are eternal pleasures." By Christ's grace, those who believe and trust in Him are set upon the path that leads to eternal life. And as we walk along this path, we walk with the presence of God, who fills us with abundant joy and eternal pleasure. Therefore, let us not settle for fleeting joy when God gives us abundant joy. Let us not seek after momentary pleasure when there is eternal pleasure in Christ.

We respond to the joy and pleasures we receive through Christ by fearing the Lord and walking in His ways. However, because of our sin nature, we can still wander down the same paths as Solomon in search of satisfaction. As Solomon has shown us, these paths will only lead us into discouragement and despair. But when the pursuits of this world leave us empty, we can turn to Jesus and be filled with His grace.

Instead of wandering down paths that will not satisfy, let us follow our Shepherd, who leads us down the path of life. Let us heed the gentle guidance of His staff that keeps us secure. Let us listen to His voice over the voices of this world that seek to pull us down futile roads. In our Shepherd, we have all we need, so let us rest in Him.

study questions

Read Psalm 23. How does this psalm remind you of what you possess in Christ? How should you respond to your Shepherd?

_____

_____

_____

_____

_____

study questions

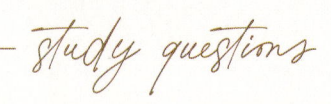

How does the gospel encourage our fear of the Lord and obedience to His commands?

How can you rest in Christ when you yearn for satisfaction and security?

Notes

Scripture Memory

week three day six

When all has been heard, the conclusion of the matter is this: fear God and keep his commands, because this is for all humanity.

ECCLESIASTES 12:13

Week Three *Reflection*

Summarize the main points from this week's passages.

_____
_____
_____
_____
_____

What did you observe from this week's text about God and His character?

_____
_____
_____
_____
_____

What did these passages teach you about the condition of mankind and yourself?

_____
_____
_____
_____
_____
_____

READ ECCLESIASTES 8:1–12:14

How did these passages point to the gospel?

How should you respond to these passages?
What specific action steps can you take this week to apply them in your life?

Write a prayer in response to your study of God's Word. Adore God for who He is, confess sins He revealed in your own life, ask Him to empower you to walk in obedience, and pray for anyone who comes to mind as you study.

Solomon's failure points to the true man of peace, Jesus.

extra

Solomon as a Type of Christ

Scripture contains numerous examples of typology. Typology is when a person, place, or object represents or foreshadows Jesus. These people, places, or things can be identified as "types" of Christ who ultimately point us to the work of Jesus Christ Himself. One of these types is Solomon. Solomon is a type of Christ in four different ways—because of his name, wisdom, works, and kingdom.

NAME

In 1 Chronicles 22:9, God promised David, "a son will be born to you; he will be a man of rest. I will give him rest from all his surrounding enemies, for his name will be Solomon, and I will give peace and quiet to Israel during his reign." Solomon's name means "Man of Peace," and we see Solomon fulfill the meaning of his name and God's promise when he became king. Through the help of the Lord, Solomon brought rest to the people of Israel. For the majority of his reign, the people of Israel did not have conflicts with enemy nations. However, Solomon soon turned away from the Lord and began worshiping false gods. God punished Solomon by promising to tear the kingdom away from Solomon's son. Even though Solomon remained king, God sent enemies upon Israel as punishment. Because of Solomon's disobedience, he forfeited the peace Israel possessed and failed to be the man of peace.

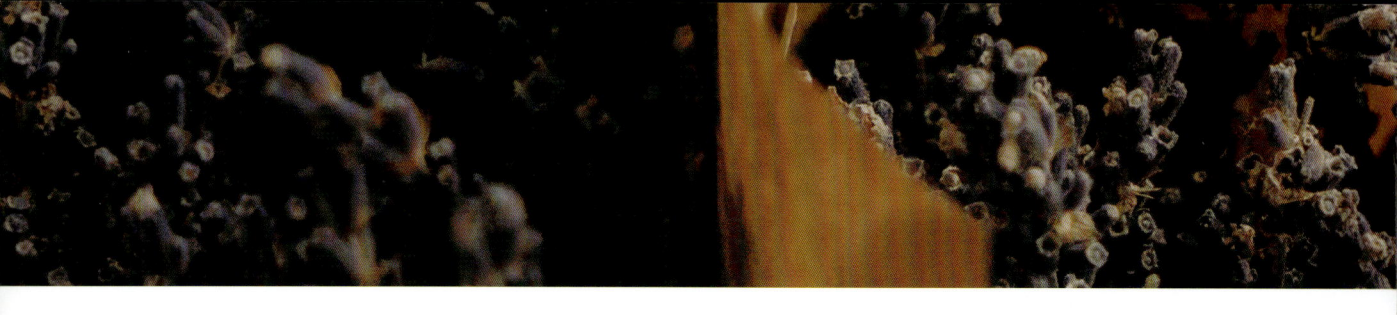

Yet Solomon's failure points to the true man of peace, Jesus. Jesus is the bringer of true and lasting peace. Through His death and resurrection, Jesus's forgiveness covers the punishment of sin, allowing those who trust and believe in Him to receive peace from God. Though the world is broken because of sin, Jesus will one day return to bring lasting peace to the earth. He will establish a kingdom of eternal rest where all believers will gather to experience everlasting peace.

WISDOM

Out of all the people in Scripture, Solomon is known to be the wisest. When God asked Solomon what he wanted, Solomon asked for a heart of wisdom (1 Kings 3:1–15). God fulfilled Solomon's request, and Solomon's wisdom became great and well-known throughout the nations. Many people, including the Queen of Sheba, came to listen to Solomon's wisdom and witness this great king of insight. Solomon reigned in wisdom as long as he walked with the Lord and was faithful to Him. However, Solomon allowed his heart to overrule his mind and broke God's command not to have relations with non-Israelite women.

Solomon's disobedience reveals his inability to be a lasting man of wisdom. Solomon's wisdom was great, but Jesus is the epitome of wisdom. Though Solomon spoke many words of wise counsel, it is only the wisdom of Christ that leads to eternal life. Solomon's wisdom was limited, but Jesus's wisdom is limitless. By His grace, Jesus imparts His wisdom to believers. Those who trust and believe in Jesus receive a heart of wisdom and the ability to walk in wisdom through the power of the Spirit.

WORKS

Solomon completed many great works during his reign, but the greatest work he accomplished was the temple. Solomon's father, David, desired to build a temple for the Lord, but God gave Solomon the task of building the temple. Solomon followed through with his father's plans, and the temple was built. The temple became a place where God's presence would dwell and where the Israelites could come to worship Him. Solomon's temple was known to be grand and beautiful, and it became a treasured place for the people of Israel. However, when Solomon's son disobeyed the Lord, God punished Israel by allowing Babylon to take the city. Sadly, the temple was destroyed by Babylon. Solomon's ruined temple points us to Jesus, who is the fulfillment of the temple, meaning He dwells with us as God dwelled in the temple.

Because Jesus is God, He brought the presence of God to earth in a new way by becoming human and dwelling with mankind. Not only this, but by Christ's sacrifice, Jesus broke the barrier sin created that separated man from God, allowing those who believe in Him to experience limitless worship to God. Those who believe in Christ also receive the Holy Spirit and are considered the new temple because of the presence of God within them. When Christ returns to establish the new heaven and new earth, there will be no need for a temple because the Lord God the Almighty and the Lamb will be its temple (Revelation 21:22).

KINGDOM

Solomon inherited the throne after David passed. Like his father, Solomon cared about uniting the kingdom of Israel and exhorting the people to walk in the ways of the Lord. Solomon's wisdom and works contributed to the expansion of the kingdom, and Israel thrived under his rule. However, Solomon's disobedience to God's commands led to the nation of Israel's ruin. After Solomon's death, Solomon's son Rehoboam did what was wrong in the eyes of the Lord, and his foolishness caused the nation of Israel to divide. The once-united and thriving kingdom of Israel was separated, vulnerable, and weak. The failure of Solomon to uphold the kingdom points us to King Jesus, whose kingdom will never end. God promised David that an offspring would come from his line who would reign over an eternal kingdom (2 Samuel 7:12–13). Yet this person ultimately was not Solomon—it is Christ.

During His earthly ministry, Jesus Himself declared, "something greater than Solomon is here" (Matthew 12:42). Though Solomon was a great king, Jesus is a far greater King. Jesus is a King who rules with perfect justice and righteousness. Where Solomon faltered, Jesus is faithful. The faithfulness and obedience of Christ led Him to the cross, where He sacrificed Himself to forgive sinners of their sins. Those who repent and trust in Jesus are brought into the kingdom of God and dedicate their lives in joyful submission to their King. One day, Jesus will return to bring the fullness of God's kingdom to earth, where He will rule with perfect righteousness forever. While the world may not recognize Jesus as King, Jesus rules and reigns over all creation. Jesus is the one true King whose kingdom never ends.

> " Jesus is the one true King whose kingdom never ends. "

What is *the* Gospel?

Thank you for reading and enjoying this study with us! We are abundantly grateful for the Word of God, the instruction we glean from it, and the ever-growing understanding it provides for us of God's character. We are also thankful that Scripture continually points to one thing in innumerable ways: the gospel.

We remember our brokenness when we read about the fall of Adam and Eve in the garden of Eden (Genesis 3), where sin entered into a perfect world and maimed it. We remember the necessity that something innocent must die to pay for our sin when we read about the atoning sacrifices in the Old Testament. We read that we have all sinned and fallen short of the glory of God (Romans 3:23) and that the penalty for our brokenness, the wages of our sin, is death (Romans 6:23). We all need grace and mercy, but most importantly, we all need a Savior.

We consider the goodness of God when we realize that He did not plan to leave us in this dire state. We see His promise to buy us back from the clutches of sin and death in Genesis 3:15. And we see that promise accomplished with Jesus Christ on the cross. Jesus Christ knew no sin yet became sin so that we might become righteous through His sacrifice (2 Corinthians 5:21). Jesus was tempted in every way that we are and lived sinlessly. He was reviled yet still yielded Himself for our sake, that we may have life abundant in Him. Jesus lived the perfect life that we could not live and died the death that we deserved.

The gospel is profound yet simple. There are many mysteries in it that we will never understand this side of heaven, but there is still overwhelming weight to its implications in this life. The gospel tells of our sinfulness and God's goodness and a gracious gift that compels a response. We are saved by grace through faith, which means that we rest with faith in the grace that Jesus Christ displayed on the cross (Ephesians 2:8–9). We cannot save ourselves from our brokenness or do any amount of good works to merit God's favor. Still, we can have faith that what Jesus accomplished in His death, burial, and resurrection was more than enough for our salvation and our eternal delight. When we accept God, we are commanded to die to ourselves and our sinful desires and live a life worthy of the calling we have received (Ephesians 4:1). The gospel compels us to be sanctified, and in so doing, we are conformed to the likeness of Christ Himself. This is hope. This is redemption. This is the gospel.

Scriptures to Reference

GENESIS 3:15

I will put hostility between you and the woman, and between your offspring and her offspring. He will strike your head, and you will strike his heel.

ROMANS 3:23

For all have sinned and fall short of the glory of God.

ROMANS 6:23

For the wages of sin is death, but the gift of God is eternal life in Christ Jesus our Lord.

2 CORINTHIANS 5:21

He made the one who did not know sin to be sin for us, so that in him we might become the righteousness of God.

EPHESIANS 2:8-9

For you are saved by grace through faith, and this is not from yourselves; it is God's gift—not from works, so that no one can boast.

EPHESIANS 4:1-3

Therefore I, the prisoner in the Lord, urge you to walk worthy of the calling you have received, with all humility and gentleness, with patience, bearing with one another in love, making every effort to keep the unity of the Spirit through the bond of peace.

> Ultimately, the path to life is found in Jesus Christ.

BIBLIOGRAPHY

McGraw, Tim. "Live Like You Were Dying." MP3 Audio. Track 5 on *Live Like You Were Dying*. Curb Records, Inc. 2004. https://open.spotify.com/album/0os-1Gz3XMM6dduZSMxVuXs?si=IS4gc2agS4axMOZOuFIOPg.

Thank you for studying
God's Word with us!

CONNECT WITH US
@thedailygraceco
@dailygracepodcast

CONTACT US
info@thedailygraceco.com

SHARE
#thedailygraceco

VISIT US ONLINE
www.thedailygraceco.com

MORE DAILY GRACE
The Daily Grace App
Daily Grace Podcast